D0143025

# RAPE AND
# THE LIMITS OF
# LAW REFORM

# RAPE AND THE LIMITS OF LAW REFORM

**Jeanne C. Marsh**
*University of Chicago*

**Alison Geist**
*University of Michigan*

**Nathan Caplan**
*University of Michigan*

 *Auburn House Publishing Company*
*Boston, Massachusetts*

091671

*Library of Congress Cataloging in Publication Data*
Marsh, Jeanne C., 1948–
   Rape and the Limits of Law Reform

   Includes index.
   1. Rape—United States.  I. Geist, Alison.
II. Caplan, Nathan.  III. Title.
KF9329.M37      364.1′532      81–20621
ISBN 0–86569–083–9          AACR2

Printed in the United States of America

*To the Michigan Women's Task Force on Rape*

# FOREWORD

When the model rape reform law was passed in Michigan in 1974, women working to combat rape hoped it heralded a new era for victims everywhere. By 1975 many believed that, especially in the nations' big cities, police and emergency medical personnel had markedly improved their treatment of, if not their attitudes toward, victims, and that the courts were the last major institutional bastion that needed to be changed if victims were ever to receive just treatment and genuine help in the apprehension and prosecution of their attackers. By the late 1970's, when the impact of the new law in Michigan was beginning to be felt, hundreds of thousands of women were participating in "take back the night" marches organized throughout the country by the National Organization of Women. In many of the marches chants of "Take Back the Night" were accompanied by cries of "Stop Rape, Now!" symbolizing women's recognition of their right to move freely in their communities without fear of being raped. The marches also served notice that women are taking measures to bring about changes which will allow them that freedom. This book, which documents the development, implementation, and initial impact of the Michigan law, suggests what help women can expect from legal reform in many other states as the battle continues.

Other treatises on rape and the law have been devoted to articulations of the differences among state laws, requirements for successful prosecution of rape cases, and varying penalties associated with "degrees" of the crime. While not ignoring these topics, this book contributes also to our understanding of the effectiveness of the new laws as a mechanism for promoting social reform, the functioning of professionals in bureaucratic and technical environments, and the complex relationship between attitudes and behaviors.

## Legal Reform and Social Change

The story of the development and passage of the Michigan law, expected at the outset to be a model for other states, is also a story of negotiation and compromise. Since rape is not a federal crime but one governed by state laws, the battle for reform—if there is to be wide-spread reform—will have to be fought in every state. Just a few years ago several states had laws requiring the death penalty for convictions in rape cases. Believing such an extreme penalty inhibited convictions, reformists in some of these states were in the anomalous position of lobbying for new laws with reduced penalties in order to increase the likelihood that juries would convict. The variations in existing law and differing constellations of personalities and vested interests mean that the negotiations, compromises, and outcomes all will differ.

However, the Michigan experience reminds us that the people who make laws are elected, and are usually men. Further, we are reminded, the legal process in our nation is designed to protect the innocent; persons who have been apprehended and charged with rape are not rapists until proved so. Laws against rape therefore reflect what elected male legislators believe should be required to prove a man (usually) guilty of the crime. Although there may be agreement on the correctness of prosecuting in the case of a brutal stranger rape, legislative debate over issues of marital rape, acquaintance rape, rape without other extensive physical damage, and the relevance of the victim's sexual conduct tap basic—almost primordial—beliefs about the subservient place and role of women, sex, seduction, and fear. Increasing public support for reform puts an important countervailing pressure on many of these male legislators, leading to discrepancies which may cause them to take publicly pro-reform actions while nonetheless holding onto outdated myths and perceptions. This situation suggests the need for both community education and legislative reform efforts to go hand in hand.

A question raised by the authors is whether the changes in law can be used to bring about reform or whether the laws reflect societal change which has already taken place. The answer from Michigan is mixed.

## Reform and Change

The enactment and implementation of the Michigan law were expected to affect victims, actors in the legal system, and perhaps perpetrators of future rapes. The experience in that state indicates that the reform brought about changes in procedure but not in basic attitudes or definitions of the crime.

Passage and implementation did not seem to result in fewer rapes; thus one may infer that greater likelihood of conviction did not inhibit rapists. Procedural changes resulting in more efficient and successful prosecutions did not seem to be accompanied by changes in the attitudes of police, attorneys, or judges, although it is possible that jurors were affected. Victims were reported to be less traumatized by the judicial system experience under the new law and to be more willing to follow through on prosecution. The authors say that this willingness to prosecute, however, may also be attributable to a consciousness-raising of women in the general public resulting in a more widespread belief that rape is not the victim's fault. Thus, it would seem that, although there was reform, there was not real change, or at least that it is still unmeasureable. We can hope that ultimately the altered procedures and accompanying behavior will lead to permanent, more complete change.

## Lawyers, Processing Cases, and Winning

In many, if not all, rape cases the victim is merely a witness and the man charged with rape is accused of committing a crime against the state. The state has a "good" case against the accused insofar as the victim (usually the only witness) can identify the assailant and there is evidence (provided by the victim) of penetration, of use of force or the threat of force, and of the fact that it was against her will. Given the circumstances of many rapes, it is often difficult for victims to provide convincing evidence on all of these points, especially the last.

Although the activists in Michigan, as they worked for reform, may have thought they were working solely to improve conditions for victims, the new law also improved conditions for people working in the criminal justice system. New procedures made it possible for the work associated with rape cases to be more efficiently done by police and medical personnel. Further, lawyers there report that other changes—especially the elimination as relevant of the previous sexual conduct of the victim-witness— made rape easier to prove and, therefore, rape cases more winnable.

Above all, this story of the limits of the Michigan reform teaches us that the legal system is part and parcel of society. Its superior place in the hierarchy of our society's institutions does not protect it from influence of myths, fallacies, and political pressure. And, at the same time, we learn that at least some elements of even this very old system are amenable to reform. Some time ago one of the authors, Nathan Caplan, chastized his peers, noting that their exclusive attention to psychological variables made it easier for legislators to avoid the difficult and unpopular choices which could bring about real systemic change. This book focuses on the system variables and offers evidence and tools which could be used to support pro-reform legislators.

The reform in the Michigan law did at least alter procedures in a very important social system and in a way that helps victims. We can only hope that, in time, this reform will lead to a more thorough-going, permanent change and that it will spread to other important social systems. For it is only when the full weight of a range of institutions can be brought to bear that there can be generated the pressures and conditions capable of eliminating rape.

MARGARET T. GORDON
*Chair, National Advisory Committee*
*on Prevention and Control of Rape*
*Director, Center for Urban Affairs and*
*Policy Research at Northwestern*
*University*

# PREFACE

In recent years, the law has provided a means for expanded political participation by groups with relatively little power in society. Women, blacks, environmentalists, and consumers have used legislation and litigation to address injustices and to bring about social change. Jo Freeman, student of social movements and the women's rights movement in particular, has identified three conditions necessary for successful social change through the political process.* First, a law with supportive judicial interpretation must be in place that states public support for the change and that specifies explicitly the means for the change. Second, the law must be implemented and enforced by an administrative structure sympathetic to the intent of the law. And finally, the beneficiaries of the change must organize to take full advantage of the change and to exert pressure on the administrative structure to improve implementation efforts. The reciprocal influence of the law, of the administrative organization, and of the reform groups is obvious but is neither well understood nor well documented. Theories of power in America are only beginning to account for the impact of social movements and the role of law as an instrument used by these groups to promote social change. It is the purpose of this book to shed some light on these issues by examining the specific effects of one law reform premised on the values and goals of the women's rights movement: Michigan's criminal sexual conduct law. Michigan's law was one of the earliest and most comprehensive of reformed laws addressing the inadequacies in the handling of rape cases.

---

* Jo Freeman, *The Politics of the Women's Liberation Movement* (New York: David McKay Company, 1975).

The degradation of victims and the trivialization of the crime that characterized the handling of rape by the criminal justice system provided a logical target for those concerned about inequities in social conditions of women. And while the study results will provide insights with respect to the role of law reform as an instrument for social change in the women's movement, it is designed, more importantly, to document the extent to which one particular law modified the way in which this crime is handled in the criminal justice system. While the trauma of rape cannot be mitigated by a law, it is conceivable that the provisions of a law can articulate a view of the crime and procedures for handling it that will increase the possibility that the victim will be treated with respect and dignity and that the trauma of pursuing prosecution will be minimized.

There is little empirical evidence to indicate what outcomes can be expected from a change in any law. While the passage of laws has certain symbolic impact, it is unclear what instrumental impact can be expected. This study is designed to provide information about the instrumental effects of a law. Victims of rape have received particularly degrading treatment, and an evaluation of the law's effectiveness will measure its worth as an ameliorative strategy. Further, an assessment of the instrumental outcomes of Michigan's criminal sexual conduct law will provide useful information for those in other states who hope to change societal response to the crime of rape through legislative reform.

This evaluation, then, is designed to identify specific changes that can be expected from a rape law reform and to examine the dynamics of these changes as they represent the use of law reform as a tool for achieving social change. The focus is on assessing changes attributable to the law and on describing factors in the criminal justice system and the environment that may have influenced these changes. Implementation of the law as well as its impact are examined to enhance understanding of measured changes. While the impact of the law reform is tested and factors contributing to social change are described, it is premature in this study to attempt to test specific theories of social change.

In the early chapters of the book, we examine the actual effects of the law reform. After describing the background and specific provisions of the law reform in Michigan in Chapters 1 and 2, we discuss the impact of the law on crime statistics (reports, arrests and convictions) in Chapter 3. We examine the impact of the law as perceived by members of the criminal justice system in Chapters 4 and 5; these data both corroborate and enrich the evidence of impact provided in Chapter 3. Perceptions of police, prosecutors, defense attorneys, judges, and crisis center counselors provide a more detailed view of what can be expected from a law reform. In Chapter 6 the characteristics of the criminal justice system that interfere with straightforward implementation of the law are described. This chapter provides a picture of what happens when a law promulgated by a social change effort is administered by a traditional institution of social control. Finally, in Chapter 7, we analyze factors outside the criminal justice system that influence and facilitate activities inside the system.

## Methodology

The primary research methodologies in this study were (1) time series analysis of crime statistics and (2) structured interviews with criminal justice officials and rape crisis counselors. Although it is less true today, at the beginning of the study there was a paucity of theoretical or descriptive information to enhance our understanding of the handling of sexual assault cases or the type and level of impact that could be expected from a law change. As a result, we had little theoretical or experiential knowledge to guide the design of the study. Therefore, early in the study, we engaged in a blend of data-collection techniques that included direct observation of sexual assault trials; substantial informal interviews with criminal justice officials, rape crisis counselors, and veterans of the anti-rape effort in Michigan; and reviews of relevant documents and news clippings describing the law's enactment. Through these qualitative techniques we acquired a rich, experiential base that informed the design of the study, the development of instruments, and eventually the analysis of the data. Furthermore, the structured interviews were conducted entirely by the research staff, the same individuals eventually responsible for analyzing them. Substantial incidental contextual information was acquired as a result of the researchers' direct involvement in the interviews. Information gathered in early stages of the study and during the interviews provided important background information for identifying inconsistent or incongruous facts and simplistic interpretations. The analysis of the quantitative crime statistics and the structured interviews was undoubtedly enhanced by this experience base.

## Acknowledgements

We are indebted to our colleagues, Gary Gregg, Janice Harrington, and Daniel Sharphorn, for their work with us from the conceptualization of the study design to the completion of the final report. With good humor and good sense they enhanced the sensitivity and relevance of the research. We are similarly grateful to members of the Michigan Women's Task Force on Rape, Virginia, Nordby, Jan BenDor, Barbara Timmer, and Carole Living, for sharing their experiences. Numerous others—including Lynn Levin, Cathy McCleary, Jody Bisdee, John Broder, Barbara Parker, and David Patterson—contributed energy and insight to the effort. Finally, we thank respondents of the study who shared their observations and ideas, as well as those individuals who provided help in arranging interviews and obtaining crime statistics: Stephen Boake of the Wayne County Prosecutor's Office, Lieutenant James Cofell of the Detroit Sex Crimes Unit, and Colonel Gerald Hough and Richard Hintz of the Michigan State Police. Over the course of the study an unusually talented and forebearing group of individuals provided secretarial support. We wish to thank Bonnie Frank and Kathy Bosirico. The final manuscript was meticulously completed by Gwendolyn Graham. Support for the study was provided by Grant MH 29532 from the National Center for the Prevention and Control of Rape, the National Institute of Mental Health; additional support was provided by the School of Social Service Administration, the University of Chicago.

# CONTENTS

# LIST OF TABLES

*Chapter 1*

# THE ROLE OF LAW REFORM

In a variety of ways in the past twenty years, women have been expressing a desire for a change in the structure and reward system of society. Activities related to the expression of these preferences, the women's rights movement, have focused on a number of issues, which include substantial concern with the crime of rape. Concern has been with reducing the frequency of this rapidly escalating crime, whose primary victims are women, and with eliminating procedures used to handle rape cases that are unlike those used for other violent crimes. Traditional procedures are mired in assumptions inconsistent with the realities of the crime and the activities of women in society today.

## Women's Rights, Rape, and the Law Reform Solution

The inequities in the processing of rape cases have been widely articulated. Victims are often discouraged from reporting and prosecuting cases because of humiliating and degrading treatment by hospital staff, police officers, prosecutors, defense attorneys, and judges. Many victims suffer great physical and psychological trauma from the rape, but they can expect to be retraumatized by the criminal justice system. They must prove that they did not consent by demonstrating resistance "to the utmost," or they may have to describe their entire sexual history in order to prove that they have never engaged in nontraditional sexual

1

activity. Most state laws rest on assumptions such as the following: that the woman invited the attack by her appearance and behavior; that previous sexual activity implies consent to subsequent encounters, no matter how violent; and that previous sexual contact is tantamount to continuing acquiescence. Indeed, no other crime is so fraught with assumptions and rigorous standards of nonconsent.

As with any social issue, numerous strategies have emerged to address the problem of rape. Crisis centers have been established to aid victims and educate the public. Rape evidence kits have been distributed to law enforcement agencies to insure that evidence in sexual assault cases is secured properly. Demonstrations, educational campaigns, speak-outs, and court cases have brought the risks and realities of rape to public attention. But legislative reform has remained the social change strategy of choice. From the earliest articulation of the problem, it was argued that antiquated statutes provided little protection for the victim and hindered effective prosecution.

The rapidly increasing use of law as a mechanism of political participation is a notable development in recent legal and social history.[1] Diverse groups, including blacks, welfare rights organizations, environmentalists, consumer groups, and women, have used the law to promote changes they desired. Through the efforts of the legal arms of social movement groups (such as the NAACP Legal Defense Fund) as well as government- or foundation-funded legal service programs (such as the legal service programs of the Office of Economic Opportunity or the Ford Foundation), the law has become an alternative mechanism of political participation. That is to say, it is no longer simply a means for asserting individual claims before a recognized and accepted authority. Rather it has become a means by which groups and organizations can participate in the determination of public policy. Expanded legal participation is a hallmark of what Nonet and Selznick have labeled "responsive law."[2]

Michigan's criminal sexual conduct law, which took effect in April 1975, is considered to be the most innovative and far-reaching legislation in the area of rape.[3] It represents a classic use of law as an instrument of social change and a major victory for groups seeking to enhance the status of women. At the time of the law reform, forcible rape was the most rapidly increasing crime of violence in the United States. While other violent crimes were decreasing between 1969 and 1975, forcible rape increased in Michigan by 56 percent.[4] In the United States between 1967 and 1977, forcible rape more than doubled from 27,620 to 63,000.[5] And while the incidence of forcible rape was escalating, very few cases were successfully prosecuted. The law reform in Michigan represents what has become a widespread approach to ameliorating this problem and addressing the broader social issues it symbolizes.

The traditional view of the crime of rape has expressed the degrading notion that women would consent to a brutal, violent assault, or that their essentially vindictive nature would lead them to fantasize about and fabricate the occurrence of the crime. This view of rape often makes victims feel responsible for causing the crime and leaves them few options for preventing it except to seek the protection of men by assuming traditional roles and patterns of behavior. Because old laws were predicated on this degrading and confining view of women, efforts to reform them represent more than a redefinition of the crime. Such efforts are part of a larger statement that, as women move into more autonomous roles in society, their activities deserve to be acknowledged and respected. Reformed rape laws, then, reflect and legitimate increasingly varied and independent roles and styles of behavior for women in society. They define the crime in terms consistent with emerging concerns of women. Bienen observes, "In the coming decade, legislative reforms in the area of rape will continue to mirror and measure the ongoing transformation of the status of American women."[6]

This book describes the impact of a model rape law reform. It examines the nature of this statute, as well as its impact and the ways in which the criminal justice system and the groups responsible for the reform facilitate or impede its implementation. The nature of reform is conceptualized in terms of three factors: the law, the system responsible for implementing it, and the groups pressing for change. In the following chapters, study findings focus on the interaction between specific provisions of the law and the criminal justice system. Then, in the final chapter, the influence of social reform groups on the implementation of the law is examined to further refine our understanding of the conditions conducive to change. The relationships among factors is examined in an effort to increase understanding of social reform generally and to predict more accurately the effect of similar rape law reforms now being adopted in more than forty states. Given the role of rape as an issue in the women's rights movement, the discussion is designed to illuminate the effectiveness of rape law reform as a strategy in the campaign to enhance women's rights.

## Law Reform as an Instrument for Social Change

Michigan's criminal sexual conduct statute held the promise of change that would be both instrumental and symbolic in impact: Properly implemented it could bring about change in the criminal justice system and the incidence of rape arrests and convictions; at the same time it could confront and change cultural norms.

The desired symbolic impact of the reform was evident when anti-rape activists in Michigan described their decision to opt for legislative reform as a *"visible* place to start the process of change."[7] Other advocates of law reform describe this perspective as follows:[8]

> *Despite the fact that rape reform legislation does not provide a total solution to the problem, it should be enacted since it will, at the very least, establish a strong policy in support of the rape victim. Such a policy should counteract the historical bias against rape victims by giving notice that the rights of the rape victim will no longer be subordinated to those of the accused.*

The reformers were less certain that the law could have an instrumental impact.

The instrumental functions of the law as expressed in the major objectives of the law reform effort were (1) to redefine and recriminalize rape and other forms of sexual assault, extending equal protection to excluded groups; (2) to bring the legal standards for rape cases in line with those used in other violent crimes by normalizing requirements for evidence; and (3) to exercise control over decisions made in the criminal justice system.[9] Uncertainty about the instrumental effect of the law is expressed by the coordinator of the Michigan Women's Task Force on Rape which drafted and lobbied for the law's passage:[10]

> *While we must have done something right to so upset the traditionalists, I would nevertheless caution the enthusiasts against the*

*belief that an untested law can be a model law. Its carefully chosen words may say what many of us want a fair law to say. But we do not yet know if in practice it will help to right what is so desperately wrong. More than a legal reform, the Michigan law is an experiment in which we hope to learn how a major revision in the criminal code can deter, control, publicize, and equalize the treatment of a very destructive set of acts against human beings.*

Law reform goals are achieved when legal provisions constrain certain behaviors or acts. The success of these efforts depends in large measure on the law and specific rule changes it attempts, as well as on the system to which it is applied. Handler[11] describes the optimal situation for accomplishing instrumental goals as existing when a legal change specifies certain procedures that must be followed in processing cases, is easily monitored, is technically simple, and reduces organizational discretion. He suggests that law reforms only rarely result in achievement of instrumental goals, and that their primary value rests in providing legitimacy and visibility to certain attitudes and values. These symbolic gains may be enough to satisfy some groups or may create the momentum required to achieve instrumental goals later. Because laws have multiple, complicated and sometimes conflicting goals that imply multiple functions for the justice system, they are often displaced by the informal expectations and desires of participants in the system. Criminal justice—in particular the judicial process —is a system in which the behavior of participants is influenced more by informal norms and expectations than by external forces.[12] While the form and substance of interactions within this system are shaped by statutes and case law as well as by organizational policies, the expectations of judges, attorneys, and police officers for each other are by far the most influential force determining case outcome. As a result of the broad discretion that exists, the system must be described and understood in terms of the objectives and perceptions of the participants. If we are to move beyond simple assessments of whether a law is successful as an instrument of social change, we must begin to describe and understand the system that implements all laws.

The criminal justice system is commonly thought to be an adversarial process dependent on binding legal rules and in which adjudication is emphasized. The culmination of a police investigation, a prosecutor's warrant for arrest, and the opposite and

competing positions taken by attorneys is a sanction consistent
with legal rules imposed by a judge or jury. In reality ". . . an
informal network of relationships is the most significant characteristic of the judicial process; most issues are negotiated rather
than adjudicated and an atmosphere of cooperation and accom-
modation rather than of explicit competition prevails. Informal
relationships exert as much or more influence than formal law."[13]
The discrepancy between formal rules and informal procedures
derives from the broad discretion employed by all participants
with respect to nearly every decision made. Laws serve as guides,
leaving specific decisions to individual interpretation and judgment. Laws themselves provide boundaries for discretion, but the
extent of influence depends on the law itself.

While the impact of a law is filtered through the bureaucratic
routines and informal interaction of the criminal justice system,
the criminal justice system itself is influenced by the environment
in which it operates. It must be accountable to the environment
on which it depends for resources and political support. This
dependence makes typically intransigent bureaucracy vulnerable
to change. When law reform is accompanied by organized efforts
to monitor implementation, it is much more likely to have an
effect. Constituency groups promoting the law reform can make a
critical contribution to its success by sustained, visible pressure on
those responsible for implementation.

## Evaluating a Law Reform

Reflecting the need to understand and document the efficacy of
law reform as a social policy instrument, the number of "legal impact" studies has increased along with the number of law reform
efforts. Legal impact studies have been plagued by problems common to the evaluation of other types of social intervention strategies—problems related to multiple goals and functions of laws,
difficulties in selecting appropriate indicators of change, and frequent failure to attend implementation issues. Several writers
have suggested that knowledge of effective reform strategies has
been reduced by studies that focus too narrowly on the law as the
independent variable and its impact on one or two indicators of
legal procedure such as crime rate, number of cases going to trial,

or number of convictions obtained.[14] Some of these writers question the feasibility of identifying, operationalizing, and measuring the goals of the law. They suggest that the vague language and multiple functions of law make it inappropriate to try to identify specific causes and effects related to law reform. Further, they suggest that the focus on a single goal or set of goals inserts serious bias into the analysis and distorts understanding of the way law influences how individuals plan and organize their behavior.

An essential aspect of these criticisms of legal impact studies is that they characteristically ignore implementation of the reform. Studies identifying specific remedies and their desired consequences without considering the process and problems of implementation within the criminal justice system are of limited value. Because they simply assess impact versus no impact, they provide no information about the contextual factors that influence the ultimate effect of a law. They provide little information about the relationships between substantive law and procedural law or between interpersonal interactions and organizational dynamics as influences on outcome. Consequently, when a particular law reform is not effective, we are often left without understanding of the dynamics of its failure. Nimmer attributes this problem to neglect of issues of implementation:[15]

> . . . the repetition of failure of reforms can be attributed in large part to recurring misperceptions about the nature of the judicial process and about how behavior within that process can be modified.

Such considerations indicate that, in addition to establishing causal relationships between laws and their effects, the evaluation of law reforms must begin to develop better conceptualizations of the nature of change through legal reform. This, of course, means focusing as much attention on the system responsible for implementing the reform and the groups responsible for passing the reform as on the reform itself. The evaluation of Michigan's criminal sexual conduct law represents an attempt to address these concerns by combining time series analysis of crime statistics with in-depth interviews with those responsible for mobilizing the machinery of the law.

In our approach to understanding the effect of Michigan's criminal sexual conduct law, interrupted time-series analysis of publicly available archival crime data was used to document in-strumental changes that could be attributed to the law.[16] In-depth interviews of individuals experienced in the implementation of the law were used to ascertain that the law had, in fact, been implemented and to give breadth to the understanding of the changes that had occurred.[17] This methodology allows access to two primary sources of information whose configuration illu-minates both the impact of the change and the process through which that impact was achieved. While crime statistics reveal the relationships between the law and, for example, arrest trends, qualitative data obtained through structured interviews, and sup-plemented by informal interviews and observation of procedure, allow us to determine whether and in what ways the law was implemented. This combination of data sources, although more complex an undertaking, not only enhances the validity of the findings but provides a richer understanding of the causes of and impediments to the law's influence.[18]

## Endnotes

1. Joel F. Handler, *Social Movements and the Legal System: A Theory of Law Reform and Social Change* (New York: Academic Press, 1978); and Philippe Nonet and Philip Selznick, *Law and Society in Transition: Toward Responsive Law* (New York: Harper and Row, 1978).
2. Nonet and Selznick, *ibid.*
3. Leigh Bienen, "Rape III—National Developments in Rape Reform Legislation," *Women's Rights Law Reporter* (1980), 6 (3), pp. 170–213.
4. Michigan State Police, *State of Michigan: Uniform Crime Report*, 1975.
5. Federal Bureau of Investigation, *Uniform Crime Reports* (1977).
6. Bienen, *op. cit.*
7. Jan BenDor, personal communication.
8. H. Sasko and D. Sesek, "Rape Reform Legislation: Is It the Solution?" *Cleveland State Law Review* (1975), 24, pp. 422–463.
9. Jan BenDor, "Justice After Rape: Legal Reform in Michigan," in Marcia Walker and Stanley Brodsky (eds.), *Sexual Assault: The Victim and the Rapist* (Lexington, Mass.: Lexington Books, 1976).
10. BenDor (1976), *op. cit.*
11. Handler, *op. cit.*
12. See Raymond T. Nimmer, *The Nature of System Change: Reform Impact in the Criminal Courts* (Chicago: American Bar Foundation, 1978).
13. Nimmer, *ibid.*, p. 38.
14. Malcolm M. Feeley, "The Concept of Laws in Social Science: A Critique and Notes on an Expanded View," *Law and Society Review*

(1976), 10, pp. 497–523; George J. McCall, *Observing the Law: Applications of Field Methods to the Study of the Criminal Justice System,* NIMH monograph, DHEW Publication no. (ADM) 76–246 (1976); and Nimmer (1978), *op. cit.*

15. Nimmer, *op. cit.,* p. 2.

16. Uniform Crime Report data for forcible rape (CSC1) were obtained from the Michigan State Police for the period January 1972 through December 1978. These data provide evidence of trends before and after the law reform in reports, arrests, and convictions. To determine trends in less serious sexual assault crimes, records for all sexual assault crimes (CSC1, 2, 3, 4) processed between August 1975 and May 1979 were obtained from the Detroit Police Department's Sex Crimes Unit.

17. The data base for assessing the implementation of the law was the structured interview survey of members of the criminal justice system and assault or rape crisis center staff in six counties in southern Michigan. The sample for the structured interviews was a purposive sample of thirty-four judges, forty prosecutors, thirty-one defense attorneys, thirty-nine police officers, and twenty-six crisis center staff from six counties who, with the exception of some members of the latter group, had experience with sexual assault cases before and after the law reform. The six counties in the sample were selected for their heterogeneity. While all six were among the thirteen counties in the state with the highest sexual assault rate, they included a large metropolitan county with the highest crime rate in the state, a small rural county (the only lower peninsula county without a sexual assault crisis center), and a county containing a large university campus. Given this sampling strategy, the task of the analysis was to determine whether the law reform was implemented in comparable ways in each county. County differences, where notable, will be identified in the discussion of findings.

The structured interviews took place between July and October 1978. All interviews were conducted by six primary research staff. Because these individuals were involved in the design of the study and development of the interview instruments, training focused on obtaining consistency in interviewing procedures.

Five structured interview schedules were employed, one for each group of respondents. Each interview schedule contained questions common to all respondents and some tailored for particular respondent groups. A sample interview schedule designed for prosecutors is provided in Appendix A.

18. Jeanne C. Marsh, "Combining Time Series and Interview Data: Evaluating a Sexual Assault Law," in Ross F. Conner (ed.), *Methodological Advances in Evaluation Research* (Beverly Hills: Sage, 1981).

*Chapter 2*

# PASSAGE AND PROVISIONS OF A LEGAL INNOVATION

The Michigan rape law reform passed the legislature in record time. Only five months elapsed between its introduction and passage.[1] This success was remarkable because, with its passage, a few concerned women substantially altered the legal definition of rape even before the national anti-rape movement emerged.

Lessons learned from this important experience can be extrapolated to other states and other social change efforts premised on law reform. For this reason, it is relevant to document the events surrounding passage of the law. In 1973 the Michigan Women's Task Force on Rape formed a bipartisan coalition of women's groups and law-and-order advocates and effectively mobilized the expanding network of feminists in the state. In bringing about a radical departure from a centuries-old approach to rape, the law reformers agreed that providence was nearly as important as expertise.

## Formation of the Women's Task Force on Rape

Anti-rape activities began in Michigan long before the pursuit of the law reform strategy and are closely tied to the emergence of the women's movement in the 1960s and 1970s. A series of brutal rapes in Ann Arbor mobilized feminists there to form the Women's Crisis Center[2] in 1971. Operating out of a member's basement, the

11

"hot line" was to be the first step in providing medical assistance and emotional support for victims of rape. But until April of 1972 not one rape victim called. Instead women were telephoning for assistance in identifying a source of safe abortions, which at that time were illegal in most of the United States. Concern about rape was overshadowed by a compelling need for safe abortions. Consequently, the Women's Crisis Center became Women's Liberation Abortion Counseling, setting the rape issue aside until the U.S. Supreme Court ruling in January 1973 made abortions legal in all states.

In the process of achieving legalization of abortion, women had become accomplished organizers. Nationally their approach— later to characterize the anti-rape movement—grew from counseling a few individuals to seeking intervention by the courts on behalf of many.

Since abortion rights no longer dominated the "women's issues" agenda, Ann Arbor feminists again turned their attention to the alarming rape rates and the traumatic sequelae of the crime. The Women's Crisis Center (WCC) was a locally focused collective, but its history is not unlike that of many centers across the nation. The members' objective was to provide supportive counseling for victims of rape and simultaneously to expose the myths that had prevented effective approaches to dealing with this violent crime.

To augment the scarce statistics collected by law enforcement agencies, the WCC conducted a local victimization survey. Its immediate goal was to provide data about the number and nature of rapes in the area to convince police and hospital personnel of the need for better services. One hundred fifty victims called, including many who had not initially reported the assault to authorities.

The women who responded were predominantly white and had most frequently been attacked in and around their homes by white assailants. The findings confirmed a point activists had argued for some time: that the stereotypical "back alley" rapes account for a small percentage of sexual assaults. The study results were combined with a literature review in a fifteen-page pamphlet, *Freedom From Rape*. Advertising in feminist publications, the WCC received 20,000 requests for reprints from all over the country. Awareness of rape was growing.

The Center had developed a program of rape counseling that sometimes—but not always—involved the criminal justice system when the victim wished to prosecute. Initially, alternative counseling services were offered to victims because the insensitivity of police and hospital staff was actually a barrier to reporting and successful prosecution. But many cases demanded participation by those authorities, and the WCC developed relationships with the criminal justice system that included both confrontation and cooperation. Police and prosecutors soon learned that victims who had received counseling were often well prepared psychologically for the ordeal of a trial; and they made better witnesses.

In 1973–1974 the relationship between the Women's Crisis Center and the criminal justice system was strengthened when Ann Arbor's City Council approved funds to create the Community Anti-Rape Effort and to house it in City Hall. The successful appeal for assistance was couched in "law and order" language, and thus Michigan's anti-rape activists began a lasting but delicate alliance with established authority. The Community Anti-Rape Effort eventually became the Assault Crisis Center, which still serves the area. A cooperative relationship with existing structures was fairly assured; the Center was officially part of the bureaucracy. Anti-rape activities had most certainly gained legitimacy. But some observers felt that activists had bargained away a valuable asset in the process: the autonomy to confront the criminal justice system directly.

Despite their success, those who worked with rape victims continued to experience frustration in their brushes with the criminal justice system. In June of 1973 a group of women from southeastern Michigan rape crisis projects met at the home of Jan BenDor in Ann Arbor to discuss strategies for accomplishing more. Writes BenDor:[3]

> It appeared to us as if "carnal knowledge"—that narrowly defined band out of the wide spectrum we call rape—had in effect been de-criminalized . . . . Protesting the fact of this free crime to prosecutors and police had sent us on a chase from one buck-passing part of the system to another. They all said, "It's the law." So, although we knew that the "law" was merely the cover for 118 years of travestied justice, we determined that it was a fine place to start the process of change.

## Formation of Coalitions

Not all of those present at the initial meeting were convinced that law reform would be the appropriate avenue for change. Several radical feminists dissociated themselves from this effort, questioning the efficacy of a social change strategy to be implemented by a male-dominated institution. The remaining group became the Michigan Women's Task Force on Rape, which then contacted Virginia Nordby. Nordby, a lecturer at the University of Michigan Law School, had experience with drafting legal language. An ambitious proposal was drawn up and Task Force members began a series of meetings with the Michigan House of Representatives Judiciary Committee, while fortuitous events nudged the proposed legislation closer to reality.

In the Michigan Senate Gary Byker, a Republican, became the sponsor of Senate Bill 1207 in response to a newspaper article written by a woman reporter who had covered a presentation by BenDor on the proposed legislation. He was prodded by a letter from a constituent whose retarded child had been raped. The letter detailed the agonizing fruitlessness of pursuing prosecution under existing laws.

The bill gained a sponsor in the House in a dramatic meeting. The proposed legislation was outlined at a rape education conference, where the speaker noted that it needed another sponsor. Democratic Representative Earl Nelson was in the audience. He stood up to announce that he would sponsor the legislation in the House. The bill was thus introduced by a white Republican senator and a black Democratic representative, a bipartisan effort which was critical to the bill's success.

In early February 1974, after several unproductive meetings with the House Judiciary Committee, the Task Force held a press conference. Their public announcement of House Bill 5802 and Senate Bill 1207 coincided with the first showing of "A Case of Rape" on network television. Now considered a classic, the movie was the first widely viewed portrayal of a rape victim's ordeal in the court system. In retrospect, law reformers cite attention given to rape by the media as critical to the creation of a climate in which rape law reform could take place in Michigan.

## Mobilization of Support

While the tenor of the times was supportive, political strategies were crucial. The Judiciary Committee was stalling on the bill, and many of its members were enmeshed in primary campaigns. Task Force members converted the election year into an asset by mobilizing concerned people through a newsletter, begun at the outset of the effort. Legislators began to receive a steady flow of correspondence supporting the bill. Additionally, in March Michigan's popular Republican governor, William Milliken, publicly supported the bill's passage. The Task Force had decided very early to try to win the law's passage with a "carrot" strategy. Legislators were told that a vote for the bill would ensure votes from constituents in the primaries. Meanwhile, the chairman of the House committee was replaced; his successor proved to be more congenial to the bill.

But meetings between the Task Force and committee members were often heated. In private, legislators expressed fear of false accusation and talked at length about seductresses, orgies, blackmail, "barroom floozies," and "vindictive wives." In public, they were less apt to reveal these fears than to attack the complexity of the proposed law, the possibility that it was unconstitutionally vague, and the consequences of reducing the age of consent. But the concern over "vindictive wives" was to surface repeatedly.

As Nordby had drafted it, the law would allow spouses to file charges of rape. On April 23, at a well-attended joint hearing on the bill, the Task Force learned that members of the committee were studying a substitute drafted by a Senate Judiciary Committee lawyer. In this version, the sexual history evidentiary section and spousal protection clause had been excised. One senator said that if spouses could charge rape, married women would use the law in divorce proceedings in order to win property settlements, and that such a provision would discourage reconciliation. Responded Nordby, "I wasn't aware that rape was a form of reconciliation." Although the evidentiary section and protection for separated spouses were eventually reinstated, Task Force members compromised and accepted the spousal exclusion in order to win passage of the rest of the bill.

In late May a weakened version of the bill hit the Senate floor for a vote. Accompanying copies of the legislation on the senators' desks were letters from the Michigan Prosecuting Attorneys Association which blasted the bill. Chief Prosecutor Terry Boyle of Recorders Court in Detroit and Wayne County (Detroit) Prosecutor William Cahalan, objected to the law because, they maintained, it would hamper prosecution and conviction. A Detroit newspaper carried the story and headlined it "Cahalan Sees Bill as Boon to Rapists."

Later, Task Force members met with several prosecutors who opposed the bill and were able to convince them that, because the legislature was likely to pass some sort of bill, it would behoove prosecutors to work for the legislation while they could still influence its design. Boyle eventually became an important ally of the law reform effort.

On May 30 the *Detroit Free Press* editorialized, "With both the number of rapes and the violence connected with them on the increase, legislators have responsibility to do something about it. Senate Bill 1207 gives them an opportunity." *The Free Press* argued for the inclusion of sections dropped by the House Judiciary Committee and included a gentle nudge, ". . . (its) passage would make Michigan a leader in such overdue revision." On June 6 the weakened version of S.B. 1207 passed the Senate 30 to 1 in round-robin voting as Task Force members and lobbyists pulled senators in for the vote.

The real work was done in the House, where Task Force members adopted a strategy to appease their opponents and later to resurrect those portions of the bill lost in the Senate. This simplified the amending process, and the Task Force could plan to get the bill through committee and gut the objectionable sections later. The bill was referred to the House Judiciary Committee, where it had the support of a key legislator. But when the draft of H.B. 5802 was prepared, this legislator held a press conference to claim credit for the law. And meanwhile, Task Force members could not get a copy of the latest version. Eventually they had only half an hour to study it before the committee vote was scheduled.

The bill under consideration was again a weakened version including a suppression-of-evidence section that Task Force members had never seen before. They realized that this addition, if referred to the Conference Committee, could bottle up the bill indefinitely. Nordby and a prosecutor who had helped to draft the version Task Force members supported gave testimony on the bill while others lobbied to strike the new section. Amendments to strengthen the bill were drafted, but eventually the weakened version was passed out of committee. From there, moving into the last three days of the session, the bill's House sponsor, Nelson, took over its management.

House members continued to have reservations about the bill. Several objected to the mandatory minimum sentences provided for; others claimed that passage of that portion of the bill prohibiting sexual history information would amount to violating the separation of powers. But the Task Force had prepared papers responding to these concerns, and on July 9 the tide turned. Hal Ziegler, a Republican, had opposed the bill, representing prosecutors' interests. But he visited his district over the Independence Day recess and his constituents convinced him to support it. Ziegler gave a conversion speech that included an endorsement of the controversial evidentiary section. He maintained that the legislature should pass the bill with the section in place and allow the courts to decide if the legislature had overstepped its mandate.

Meanwhile, Task Force members had personally lobbied 95 of 110 representatives. One of the bill's opponents mishandled the debate by calling the legislation a "no fault rape bill." His outburst apparently lost him a number of votes that might have gone against H.B. 5802. In the end, the House voted 84–15 for the version the Task Force found acceptable.

A very short time remained in which to convince the Senate to concur with the House version. On July 13, the final day of the session, the Senate faced fourteen hours of business, and the rape legislation was not on the agenda. Task Force members continued to lobby for the bill. More cautiously, so did the governor's office.

At 4 a.m., with only a few weary Task Force members in the gallery, there was a lull in the Senate. Senator Byker decided to bring up the bill. One senator who opposed it brought a motion to reconsider, a parliamentary trick that would have tabled the legislation at least until September. The Judiciary Committee had added forty-five amendments, and he argued that the senators had not had enough time to study it. But he could muster only nine votes. Twenty voted against reconsideration and the bill passed the Senate as amended by the House. After the motion failed, a disgruntled senator looked up to the gallery where two Task Force members were the only observers and allegedly warned them to be prepared. "Ladies, we'll be back in September." On August 12, 1974 Governor Milliken signed the criminal sexual conduct statute into law.

## Politics of Law Reform

The unique political climate in Michigan at that time fostered passage of the criminal sexual conduct statute. Community interest in the issue, catalyzed by Task Force newsletters, combined with the politics of an election year to make the bill an attractive one for many legislators. According to Carole Living, then an administrative assistant to Senator Byker, "There was, and still is, a strong bipartisan feminist network within the Capitol that prepared it for the bill. Legislators knew this was a popular bill." And the Michigan law reformers stress the importance of winning conservative support while avoiding excessive involvement by lawmakers perceived to be "radical."

But the credibility of the Task Force was crucial. Nordby's expertise in drafting legal language was invaluable. She and her students had exhaustively researched the legal issues and were well prepared for questions that arose. Representative Dale Warner, a member of the House Judiciary Committee, said, "Of all the issues that have come before the committee recently, rape reform has been the best researched and best presented." The resolutions of support solicited from feminist and law enforcement groups gave further weight to the law reform argument. The Task Force had "expert" legitimacy that allowed them to counter the opposition.

And much of the opposition was emotional. According to BenDor, some Senate Judiciary Committee members "were more than sexists. They were very interested in protecting a number of their own sexual fantasies." Former State Senator Lorraine Beebe, chairing a public hearing on the bill, said that in her experience, "most male legislators felt there was no such thing as rape; the woman always seduces the man" (*Detroit Free Press*, May 16, 1974). Nevertheless, the opposition was usually voiced as legal doctrine. One law reformer feels that "the legislators used common law to cover up their gut feelings." But when legal questions were raised, the Task Force had answers.

Lobbying skills and media involvement gave visibility to every vote cast by legislators. Task Force members mobilized their own constituents through the newsletter and were able to spend time with individual lawmakers. Legislators began to understand that anti-rape activists were numerous, vocal and well organized. They began to recognize that a new awareness of rape was emerging among their constituents.

Finally, Task Force members list a number of fortuitous events, chief among them the contacting of Nordby, who was accomplished in the drafting of legal language. Elaine Milliken, the governor's daughter, was in Nordby's class and took an active role in researching and lobbying for the law. Her involvement, important in its own right, influenced the governor to support the bill early. Several stubborn opponents of the bill were defeated in their reelection bids. And perhaps not coincidentally, female reporters played a role in setting the agenda for hearings on the bill.

One reformer described their success as "beginner's luck." But it was skill that allowed the Task Force to convert a political climate into a legislative reality. The product was a more humane rape law and the message that women have a voice in determining where the sanctions of justice will apply.

## Provisions of Michigan's Criminal Sexual Conduct Law

The new law was designed to pursue its essentially four goals through the following innovations: (1) a degree structure, (2) prohibition of sexual history evidence, (3) elimination of resistance and consent standards, and (4) extension of the law's coverage to previously unprotected groups. The rationale and intended effect of each of these aspects of the law is described briefly below. A more detailed discussion of these innovations is provided elsewhere.[4]

### The Degree Structure

The degree structure in Michigan's law is an explicit description of criminally assaultive sexual acts. The description is articulated in terms of four degrees assessed by the seriousness of the offense, the amount of coercion used, the infliction of personal injury, and the age and incapacitation of the victim.

There are several advantages to the degree structure. It defines and codifies a range of assaultive acts, including what under the old law were "forcible rape" ("carnal knowledge of a female through the use of force or the threat of force"), "assault with intent to commit rape," "indecent liberties," "carnal knowledge of a female ward by guardian," "incest," "debauchery of youth," and "ravishment of a female patient in an institution for the insane." The degree structure thus provides comprehensive definitions of assaultive behaviors that eliminate the overlap and omission problematic under multiple statutes. It removes the disparity between acts of penetration and molestation and describes these acts as a sequence of violent coercive behaviors.

Additionally, the specification of degrees of criminal sexual assault reflects the continuum of violence represented by sexual assault crimes and allows sanctions to be imposed that are commensurate with the seriousness of the crime. Specifically:

- Penetration and coercion that result in physical injury or extreme psychological damage constitute CSC1, first degree criminal sexual conduct, with a maximum penalty of life imprisonment.
- Penetration that results in no physical injury, typically not recognized as a crime prior to the law reform due to the absence of physical trauma, is now CSC3, third degree CSC, with a maximum penalty of fifteen years in prison.
- Acts involving sexual contact other than penetration, previously charged as assault and battery, misdemeanors, or gross indecency, are now, when they include coercion, second degree CSC (CSC2), punishable by up to fifteen years in prison.
- When coercion is not involved, criminal sexual conduct in the fourth degree (CSC4), a misdemeanor, is charged, punishable by fine or imprisonment of up to two years.

The degree structure means that if penetration and threat with a deadly weapon are involved, the charge is CSC1 whether or not physical injury or extreme psychological damage may have occurred. CSC3 is charged whenever the assault involves penetration in the absence of aggravating circumstances such as a weapon or other forms of coercion. CSC2 and CSC4 include other types of sexual contact (which are clearly described in the law), either with (CSC2) or without (CSC4) aggravating circumstances. The law clearly defines the circumstances and objective facts related to prohibited sexual acts and in this way precludes the need to address the issue of consent.

An important consequence of the codification of offenses and resulting clarification of the language is reduction in the amount of discretion that can be used by law enforcement and criminal justice officials. Under the new law, police may investigate cases they would not have pursued previously—"marginal" cases in which the victim was not injured, could not prove that she had strenuously resisted, knew the offender, or was a prostitute. Prosecutors have more guidance with respect to the appropriate charge and can advocate more charges in each case.[5] And because the degree structure is a major revision, the introduction of the law sparked training workshops for police officers. These workshops resulted in revisions of police investigations and charging procedures.

The instrumental effects of the degree structure, then, can be assessed by determining whether more and different types of cases are processed by the criminal justice system and whether more warrants for arrest are requested and issued.

## The Resistance and Consent Standards

Under Michigan's old laws, a defendant could be convicted of rape only if the prosecution demonstrated the assailant's use of force and the victim's nonconsent. Michigan courts interpreted this requirement to mean the victim had to resist "to the utmost" from "the inception to the close" of the attack.[6] This demonstration of resistance was to provide an objective test of the victim's unwillingness, or lack of consent. It has been criticized on several grounds.[7] First, rape has been the only violent crime requiring proof of resistance by the victim. Second, resistance is inconsistent with the advice of many police officers who suggest apparent compliance or efforts to distract the assailant may be more effective strategies for avoiding the attack or reducing personal injury. Finally, since the use of force implies nonconsent, it should be presumed in forcible sexual assault.

Under the new law, resistance by the victim is no longer an element of the prosecutor's proofs. Instead, the statute regards evidence of coercion used by the actor, not of the victim's unwillingness, as tantamount to nonconsent. Thus while consent still may be raised as a defense in certain situations, this modification makes the prosecution of rape cases comparable to other crimes and does not require a victim to risk death in order to have a case against the assailant. This essential shift in the burden of proof was expected to improve prosecutors' chances of achieving convictions.

## Equal Protection

A major innovation of the law was to extend protection to two groups who were effectively denied it previously. Since the law is gender-neutral, males assaulted in some manner other than "sodomy" (covered under a separate law) can prosecute under the CSC statute.[8] Legally separated spouses can now prosecute assaults by their former mates. By explicitly extending coverage to these groups, the law was expected to draw more and a larger variety of cases into the criminal justice system.

## Prohibition of Sexual History Evidence

Under previous statutes the victim's past sexual conduct was considered relevant to two issues: consent and credibility. Based on the widely criticized premise that previous sexual activity implies consent, the defense could cross-examine the victim about her sexual history and present witnesses to support the probability she consented. Similarly, evidence of past sexual conduct could be introduced to impeach the victim's credibility. In all other crimes the veracity of the victim is the only proper subject of inquiry for impeachment. Only in rape was impeachment of the witness's character, specifically evidence of unchastity, a major focus of the case. This emphasis was one of the primary obstacles to the persistence of a victim through the entire prosecution.

The CSC statute prohibits evidence of prior sexual conduct

with persons other than the accused on the basis of its irrelevance and its highly prejudicial and inflammatory nature. The expected effects were: (1) to increase a victim's willingness to make and pursue complaints and generally to improve her experience in the criminal justice system; and (2) to increase the probability of convictions.

## Summary

Forming coalitions with "law and order" legislators concerned with the increasing frequency of the crime and mobilizing state-wide support through a newsletter, the media, and intense lobbying efforts, the Michigan Task Force on Rape passed a bill in 1975 that remains the most comprehensive and innovative statute of its kind. The goals of the law were to redefine the crime, to extend coverage of the law to more types of victims, to reduce the trauma experienced by the victim, and to improve the conviction rate. The reformers pursued these goals with legal provisions that included (1) a degree structure, (2) prohibition of sexual history evidence, (3) elimination of resistance and consent standards, and (4) extension of the law's coverage to previously unprotected groups. The law's specific provisions, as well as the political strength manifested by its passage, were both important influences on its implementation and ultimate impact.

## Endnotes

1. This historical account is based upon news articles, documents, and conversations with members of the Michigan Women's Task Force on Rape and other anti-rape activists.
2. At the time rape was a topic not openly discussed; thus the word "rape" was not included in the organization's title.
3. Jan BenDor, "Justice After Rape: Legal Reform in Michigan," in Marcia Walker and Stanley Brodsky (eds.), *Sexual Assault: The Victim and the Rapist* (Lexington, Mass.: Lexington Books, 1976), p. 150.
4. See Virginia B. Nordby, "Legal Effects of Proposed Rape Reform Bills," mimeograph, April 1974; Kenneth A. Cobb and Nancy R. Schauer, "Legislative Note: Michigan's Criminal Sexual Assault Law," *Journal of Law Reform* (1974), 8, pp. 217–235; Helene Sasko and Deborah Sesek, "Rape Reform Legislation: Is It the Solution?" *Cleveland State Law Review* (1975), 24, pp. 422–463.

5. The practice of multiple charges has been criticized and will be discussed in more detail in Chapter 5.
6. Cobb and Schauer (1974), *op. cit.*
7. Cobb and Schauer (1974), *op. cit.;* Sasko and Sesek (1975), *op. cit.*
8. The legal recognition that males, too, can be sexually assaulted is a significant innovation. But since women comprise the vast majority of victims, we will frequently use the feminine pronoun "she" when referring to a victim.

*Chapter 3*

# STATISTICAL INDICATORS OF LEGAL IMPACT

Crime statistics are direct and objective measures of a law's impact, and as such they provide persuasive evidence of its impact. However, trends in reports, arrests, and convictions are susceptible to influences beyond a single legislative reform. In recent years the attention focused on rape has led some observers to speculate that social and cultural factors are primarily responsible for changes in these statistics. Record keeping and case processing policies also can confound the apparent impact of a rape law revision. Our analyses, however, show that where the criminal justice system is concerned, law reform can have a profound influence on the successful prosecution of rape cases.

After enactment of the criminal sexual conduct statute in April 1975, arrest rates improved and convictions for forcible rape increased dramatically. Using time series analyses, we found that improvements in arrest and conviction rates were influenced by the new law. Reporting trends, however, continued upward independent of it. Conviction rates for the original charge of CSC increased across the state, with a concomitant decline in the number of convictions for reduced charges. The importance of plea bargaining—the mechanism through which charges are reduced—seemed to have diminished. We investigated this phenomenon in detail only in Detroit, where we found that, since 1975, convictions in CSC cases are achieved about 70 percent of the time and for all four degrees of CSC. These crime statistics

**Table 3–1    Annual Percentage Increases in Incidence of Crimes Against the Person (1973–1977)**

| Year | Forcible Rape | Murder | Aggravated Assault | Robbery |
|------|------|------|------|------|
| 1973 | +19.0 | +12.0 | +13.0 | −3.0 |
| 1974 | +6.0 | −8.0 | +8.0 | +20.0 |
| 1975 | +3.0 | −11.0 | +4.0 | −6.0 |
| 1976 | +6.0 | −4.0 | −6.0 | −7.0 |
| 1977 | +8.0 | −15.0 | +3.0 | −21.0 |

SOURCE: Department of State Police, Uniform Crime Report for the State of Michigan, 1975 and 1977.

are powerful indicators that the law exerts at least one important and indisputable influence: It helps to achieve more convictions.

## Analysis of Trends in Crime Statistics

### Criminal Sexual Conduct Reports

In the early half of the 1970s, serious crimes increased dramatically in the United States. Michigan was no exception; serious crimes there jumped 20 percent in 1974 alone.[1] After 1974 reports of forcible rape increased at a faster rate than all other serious crimes,[2] increasing even when others were beginning to decline.[3] Table 3–1 shows that while murder, robbery, and aggravated assault showed moderate or substantial declines in the last half of the 1970s, forcible rape steadily increased.[4]

There is no simple explanation for the consistent increase in rape reports. Like all reporting statistics, it may reflect an upsurge in the incidence of the crime, in reporting rates, or both. But rape reporting rates are especially sensitive to the social environment. For myriad reasons, a victim may be deterred from reporting an attack: shame or embarrassment, fear of newspaper publicity, fear of the courtroom experience.[5] The women's movement and the "sexual revolution" may have removed some of the stigma associated with being raped, but fear of retaliation by the attacker and a desire to forget about the rape remain overriding concerns for the victim.[6] After April 1975, when the CSC statute took effect, some of the continuing increase in reports may have been due to the new law. Because it clarified the definitions of the crime and prohibited the use of the complainant's past sexual history as evidence, victims had less to fear from the criminal justice system. Simultaneously, more assault crisis centers were established, offering victims information about the law that may have encouraged reporting.

To examine this possibility, we gathered rape reporting statistics from 1972 through 1978, three years before and three years after the law took effect. The monthly pattern of reports in Figure 3–1 shows no relationship between reporting trends and enactment of the CSC statute. The time-series analysis confirms this,[7] as do interviews with respondents (to be discussed later).

A rape law reform, then, does not seem to contribute to reporting trends, either by adding an incentive to report or by decreasing the crime's incidence. These data allow us to dismiss rather easily any hope that rape law reform prevents the crime, at least in the early years of its application. And there is every reason to believe that, even if the criminal justice system is now more sensitive and women in general are more willing to report

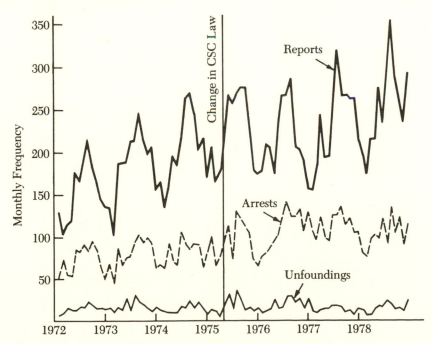

Figure 3–1  **Total monthly reports, arrests, and unfoundings for criminal sexual assault in Michigan.**

sexual assaults, many victims still may not wish to pursue prosecution. In addition to those discussed above, Dukes and Mattley identified four factors that enter into a victim's decision to report: (1) preconceived notions about police and the criminal justice system's response to rape victims; (2) the situational characteristics surrounding the rape itself; (3) the trauma suffered by the victim immediately after the assault; and (4) concerns about and advice given by family, friends, lovers, and others. In their study of both reporting and nonreporting victims, the researchers found that ". . . if conditions in any of these stages favor non-report, then the victim probably will not report the crime to police."[8] A more humane law and counseling by crisis centers may tip the scales in favor of reporting but probably cannot obliterate fear of retaliation or community disapproval.

Some critics of the law reform feared that it would increase the number of false or unjustified reports of sexual assault, wasting the authorities' time by forcing them to weed out an inordinate number of questionable cases. An examination of the unfounding rate undercuts that contention. As can be seen in Figure 3–1, unfoundings have remained stable as reports continue to increase. So the reporting trends are not a consequence of widespread public misunderstanding of the law's coverage; indeed, the same number of reports were determined to be illegitimate after the law's passage as before it.

## Criminal Sexual Conduct Arrests

In Michigan, arrests for forcible rape are increasing faster than any other crime. Between 1973 and 1977, arrests for forcible rape were up 61 percent, as compared with 16 percent increases for both murder and aggravated assault and with robbery, which showed a decline of 8 percent.[9] Table 3–2 displays these trends in more detail and supports the intuition that, with consistently increasing reports and stable frequency of unfoundings, arrests will increase at a commensurate rate.

But while reporting was not influenced by the statute, arrests apparently were. The monthly pattern of arrests for forcible rape from 1972 through 1978 (shown in Figure 3–1) reveals a relationship between arrests and the law's enactment, and this is confirmed by the time-series analysis.[10]

Table 3–2   Annual Percentage Increases in Arrests for Crimes Against the
Person (1973–1977)

| Year | Forcible Rape | Murder | Aggravated Assault | Robbery |
|------|------|------|------|------|
| 1973 | +11.0 | +32.0 | +6.0 | −2.0 |
| 1974 | +1.0 | −2.0 | +13.0 | +20.0 |
| 1975 | +17.0 | −2.0 | +5.0 | +7.0 |
| 1976 | +16.0 | +14.0 | −1.0 | −7.0 |
| 1977 | +5.0 | −19.0 | −6.0 | −21.0 |

SOURCE: Department of State Police, Uniform Crime Report for the State of Michigan, 1975 and 1977.

## Criminal Sexual Conduct Convictions

Between 1972 and 1974, the criminal justice system in Michigan achieved eight forcible rape convictions per month. Since the CSC statute was enacted, that record has improved by an average of thirteen convictions per month: From 1976 to 1978, there were twenty-one convictions per month. Of arrests, an average of 10 percent were convicted as charged before the law and 19 percent after. Both Figure 3–2 and the time-series analysis[11] show that the law contributed to the increases in conviction rates. The average number of convictions is up and there is more fluctuation over time.[12]

We also examined time-series data for convictions for lesser offenses that indicate frequency of conviction when the final charge was reduced from the original charge (for example, when a charge of CSC1 was plea-bargained to a charge of CSC3). We surmised that, as more convictions are achieved for the original charge, there would be a reduction in convictions for a lesser offense. The data, displayed in Figure 3–2, support this expectation; after the law reform there was an obvious reduction in convictions for a lesser offense.[13] Essentially, there is an inverse relationship between convictions as charged and convictions for a lesser offense after the law reform: As convictions as charged increase, convictions for a reduced charge decrease. This is true for the entire post-reform period except the latter half of 1978. Visual inspection indicates that convictions as charged and convictions for lesser offenses were both decreasing at this time. However, unlike the pre-reform pattern in which convictions for re-

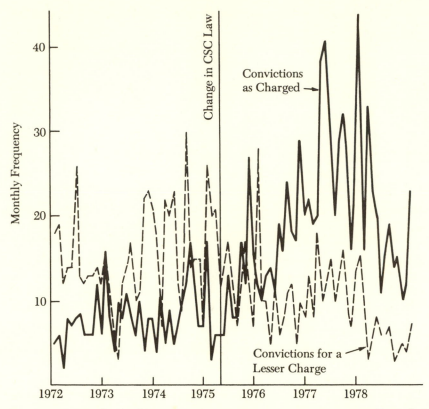

Figure 3-2   **Total monthly convictions as charged and for a lesser offense for criminal sexual assault in Michigan.**

duced charges outnumbered convictions as charged, the latter half of 1978 shows a persistence of the post-reform pattern with a slight decrease overall.[14]

## Arrest and Conviction Rates

We have been examining the actual frequency of sexual assault arrests and convictions. A similar picture emerges when we take account of reports through conventional arrest and conviction *rates* (that is, numbers of arrests and convictions *per* report). Across the nation, the conviction rate for forcible rape has always been notoriously low. LeGrand[15] used statistics from the FBI Uniform Crime Reports for the United States to calculate that in 1970 a man who raped a woman and was reported to police had roughly one chance in eight of being convicted. Other studies place the conviction rate at even lower levels. A study by the National Institute for Law Enforcement and Criminal Justice[16] calculated that approximately 2 percent of original rape complaints result in conviction. BenDor[17] calculates that in Detroit, 5 percent of 1,647 assaults reported in 1973 had resulted in conviction by plea or verdict in mid-1974.

Table 3–3 shows the arrest and conviction rates for the state of Michigan for the years 1972–1978. These data indicate that less than one-half of reported cases result in arrest. Further, they document the impact of the law by indicating some increase in the arrest rate and a notable increase in the rate of convictions as charged after the law reform. There is very little change in convictions for lesser charges. Comparable statistics based on case records obtained from criminal justice systems in Seattle and Kansas City[18] show 7 percent of original reports resulted in arrests, 2 percent resulted in convictions as charged, and 2 percent resulted in convictions for lesser charges. So comparison data from these two jurisdictions show pre-reform conviction rates in Michigan were higher to begin with and post-reform rates showed a substantial improvement on pre-reform rates.

## Effect of the Law on Each Degree of Criminal Sexual Conduct

The Michigan State Police data we have been considering provide only a partial picture of the impact of the law because they do not reveal anything about the handling of less serious sexual assault crimes. When the law was passed, there was concern that CSC3

**Table 3–3   Arrest and Conviction Rates for Criminal Sexual Conduct (1972–1978)**

| *Rates* | *1972* | *1973* | *1974* | *1975* | *1976* | *1977* | *1978* |
|---|---|---|---|---|---|---|---|
| Arrests/reports | 0.47 | 0.43 | 0.40 | 0.43 | 0.51 | 0.48 | 0.41 |
| Convictions as charged/reports | 0.04 | 0.04 | 0.05 | 0.05 | 0.08 | 0.12 | 0.07 |
| Convictions for lesser charges/reports | 0.02 | 0.01 | 0.02 | 0.01 | 0.01 | 0.01 | 0.01 |

(which includes penetration without aggravating circumstances, a crime some refer to as "date rape") and CSC4 (sexual contact without aggravating circumstances) would not be taken seriously by the criminal justice system. Because of the degree structure, there was also conjecture that the new law would foster plea bargaining, encouraging prosecutors to "charge high" in order to achieve convictions by plea. To address these concerns, we examined case records from the Detroit Police Department Sex Crimes Unit for the period January 1975 through May 1979. All of the cases for which arrests had been made during this period were included in the analysis, resulting in a total of 1,139 cases that were assessed for any differential treatment of various degrees of criminal sexual conduct. We included conviction rate, mode of processing, and disposition for each degree of criminal sexual conduct in our analysis.

## Warrants and Convictions

It would be reasonable to expect that convictions are more easily achieved for CSC1 and CSC2, cases that involve the use of force or other aggravating circumstances. CSC3 and CSC4, which represent "expanded" definitions of sexual assault, might be expected to end more readily in dismissal. The data in Table 3–4, however, suggest that approximately 70 percent of all CSC cases, no matter what the initial charge, resulted in a conviction by plea or verdict.[19] Thus, the probability of conviction does not seem to be influenced by the degree of criminal sexual assault originally charged. Unfortunately, these data provide information about case handling only after a warrant for arrest has been issued, and give no evidence of the extent to which sexual assault crimes of dif-

Table 3–4   Convictions for Each Charge of Criminal Sexual Conduct (January 1975 through December 1978)

| Initial Charge | Number | 1975 | 1976 | 1977 | 1978 |
|---|---|---|---|---|---|
| CSC1 | 817 | 72.0% | 72.1% | 71.1% | 70.9% |
| CSC2 | 138 | 84.2 | 75.0 | 77.3 | 78.4 |
| CSC3 | 139 | 72.2 | 75.9 | 61.5 | 64.9 |
| CSC4 | 45 | 75.0 | 70.0 | 69.9 | 69.2 |
| Total | 1139 | 72.9 | 73.2 | 72.8 | 70.1 |

fering seriousness are pursued after they are reported. And although convictions for each degree of CSC were equally likely to be achieved, warrants for CSC1, the most serious crime and the charge conforming most closely to traditional definitions of rape, are issued more than twice as often as warrants for CSC2, CSC3, and CSC4 combined.

The data in Table 3–5 suggest that while the original charge may not be related to the proportion of *total* convictions, it does seem to be related to whether convictions are achieved for *original charges* or for *reduced charges*. Given the latitude for plea-bargaining in CSC1 cases, we had expected that they would more often lead to convictions through charge reductions. Results in Table 3–5 indicate that, in fact, fewer CSC1 convictions were achieved with reduced charges: 58 percent for CSC1, compared with 73 percent for CSC2 and 64 percent for CSC3 charges. So, the most warrants are issued for CSC1 and the most *convictions as charged* are achieved for this crime.

In Recorder's Court in Detroit approximately 80 percent of all achieved with reduced charges: 58 percent for CSC1, compared crimes are plea-bargained at a commensurate rate, with 78 percent of CSC1 crimes, 72 percent of CSC2 crimes, 72 percent of CSC3 crimes, and 83 percent of CSC4 crimes plea-bargained. Thus, in terms of the mode of processing, each degree of CSC is handled similarly and in a manner consistent with other crimes.

## Final Dispositions

Table 3–6 displays the final disposition of the criminal sexual conduct cases investigated by the Sex Crimes Unit between 1975 and 1979. Of the 851 cases for which disposition data were available, about half resulted in prison sentences. Over 90 percent of CSC1 cases resulted in imprisonment, in contrast to 51 percent of CSC2 cases and 52 percent of CSC3 cases. Consistent with the options for a charge of CSC4 (imprisonment for not more than two years, $500 fine, or both), only 39 percent of these cases led to a jail term.

Final dispositions seem to be influenced by the mode of processing. As shown in Table 3–7, jurors are more likely to recommend imprisonment for a convicted defendant than are judges alone, and a conviction achieved through the plea-bargaining

**Table 3-5  Charge Reduction Resulting from Plea-Bargaining in Judge and Jury Trials**

| Initial Charge | Final Charge | Number | Mode of Adjudication | | | Percentage Convicted with Reduced Charge |
| --- | --- | --- | --- | --- | --- | --- |
| | | | *Plea-Bargaining* | *Judge Trial* | *Jury Trial* | |
| CSC1 | CSC1 | 223 | 66% | 12% | 22% | 58% |
| | CSC2 | 51 | 78 | 10 | 12 | |
| | CSC3 | 93 | 92 | 6 | 2 | |
| | CSC4 | 82 | 88 | 6 | 6 | |
| | Attempted CSC | 41 | 100 | — | — | |
| | Assault with intent to commit CSC | 44 | 91 | 2 | 7 | |
| CSC2 | CSC2 | 23 | 61% | 17% | 22% | 73% |
| | CSC4 | 30 | 73 | 10 | 17 | |
| | Attempted CSC | 14 | 100 | — | — | |
| | Assault with intent to commit CSC | 17 | 82 | 12 | — | |
| CSC3 | CSC3 | 29 | 59% | 10% | 31% | 64% |
| | CSC4 | 24 | 96 | — | 4 | |
| | Attempted CSC | 17 | 94 | — | 6 | |
| | Assault with intent to commit CSC | 11 | 91 | — | 9 | |
| CSC4 | CSC4 | 11 | 73% | 18% | 9% | 0% |
| Assault with intent to commit CSC | Assault with intent to commit CSC | 3 | 66 | — | 33% | |

Table 3–6    Final Dispositions of Criminal Sexual Conduct Cases Investigated Between 1975 and 1979

| Final Charge | Number | Jail | Jail and Probation | Probation |
|---|---|---|---|---|
| CSC1 | 223 | 91% | 4% | 6% |
| CSC2 | 91 | 51 | 18 | 31 |
| CSC3 | 122 | 52 | 13 | 36 |
| CSC4 | 86 | 11 | 14 | 74 |
| Attempted CSC | 72 | 27 | 12 | 62 |
| Assault with intent to commit CSC | 75 | 39 | 13 | 48 |

process is least likely to lead to jail time. When CSC2, CSC3, and CSC4 are plea-bargained, probation is usually the result. In CSC1 cases, however, probation alone is most often recommended when a judge hears the case. Juries have the least sympathy for convicted rapists, sending them to jail more often regardless of the original charge; judges are relatively more lenient.

The disposition data probably reflect attorneys' practice of reserving those cases with the strongest evidence for trial. But these statistics also challenge the assumption that jurors are unwilling to convict and seek imprisonment for CSC defendants.[21] CSC1 cases, at least, do not seem to be unusually difficult to win. And

Table 3–7    Final Dispositions Resulting from Plea-Bargaining in Judge and Jury Trials

| Final Charge | | Number | Jail | Jail and Probation | Probation |
|---|---|---|---|---|---|
| CSC1 | Plea | 147 | 88% | 5% | 7% |
| | Judge Trial | 27 | 82 | 7 | 11 |
| | Jury Trial | 49 | 100 | 0 | 0 |
| CSC2 | Plea | 72 | 42% | 19% | 39% |
| | Judge Trial | 9 | 64 | 9 | 27 |
| | Jury Trial | 10 | 60 | 30 | 10 |
| CSC3 | Plea | 102 | 51% | 11% | 37% |
| | Judge Trial | 9 | 56 | 11 | 33 |
| | Jury Trial | 11 | 58 | 17 | 25 |
| CSC4 | Plea | 73 | 9% | 14% | 77% |
| | Judge Trial | 5 | 22 | 22 | 56 |
| | Jury Trial | 8 | 25 | 25 | 50 |

jurors, free of concern about efficient case processing, may be more able than those in the criminal justice system to act upon the concern communities increasingly display toward forcible rape.

## Summary

The data from the Detroit Police Department show that convictions are likely to be achieved at the same rate for all degrees of criminal sexual assault—an astonishingly high rate of about 70 percent. But the data support the distinction respondents made between "real rape" and other forms of sexual assault. More than twice as many warrants are issued for CSC1 than for CSC2, CSC3, and CSC4 combined. While this could be due to the fact that more CSC1 crimes are committed (we have no information about this), it could also result from the fact that CSC1 crimes (which by definition are more violent and involve force, coercion, or personal injury) are more consistent with traditional understanding of rape and are therefore easier to prove.

CSC1 crimes are also more likely to result in convictions for the original charge and a disposition which involves imprisonment. Clearly, this is in part due to the violent and serious nature of CSC1 crimes. But the nonmonotonic progression of imprisonment data from CSC4 to CSC1 indicates that the difference in seriousness reflected by sentencing between CSC1 and CSC2 is considered to be much greater than that between CSC2 and CSC3, or between CSC3 and CSC4. Thus, there is a disjuncture in the perception and handling of the degrees of CSC that is not consistent with the reformer's goal of defining a "continuum of violence."

Many evaluations of social policies are based, for the most part, on determinations of whether those affected by the policy or responsible for its implementation perceive a change. This information is important, but it is more compelling when supported by objective data. Sexual assault crime data reveal the nature and extent of the law's impact, and our analyses show that a rape law reform can have a measurable influence on these statistics. Its advocates hoped that a revised rape law would make it easier for victims to report the crime and that the language of the law would enable police officers to make more arrests. Arrest rates changed somewhat and there is no evidence that the law affected reporting rates. Since most of the law's provisions govern the conduct of trials, it is reasonable to expect its greatest impact to be on conviction rates. And, indeed, the data are consistent with this expectation.

## Endnotes

1. Department of State Police, Uniform Crime Report for the State of Michigan, 1975. For a thorough discussion of the use of Uniform Crime Report statistics, see Marvin E. Wolfgang, "Uniform Crime Reports: A Critical Appraisal," *University of Pennsylvania Law Review* (1963), 111, pp. 708–738.
2. "Serious crimes" refer specifically to the seven major or "index" crimes of murder, rape, robbery, aggravated assault, burglary, larceny, and motor vehicle theft.
3. In Michigan forcible rape was covered by the "carnal knowledge" statute prior to 1975; after the reformed law was enacted in April 1975, it became criminal sexual conduct in the first degree.
4. The number of reported rapes does not begin to reflect the actual incidence of this crime. Susan Griffin in "Rape: The All American Crime," *Ramparts* (September 1971), indicated that one in ten rapes is reported; Phillip H. Ennis in a 1976 Report of the President's Commission on Law Enforcement and Administration of Justice, *Criminal Victimization in the United States: A Report of a National Survey*, concluded that 75 percent of all rapes go unreported. Using this figure, and average monthly reporting rates, over 10,000 rapes are committed each year in Michigan. The most conservative estimates of unreported rape derive from the LEAA Census Surveys which suggest that the reported/unreported ratio is comparable to that of other crimes, of which approximately half are reported. The 1972 LEAA study places the ratio of unreported rapes at 2.1 to 1.
5. See John M. MacDonald, *Rape Offenders and Their Victims* (Springfield, Ill.: Thomas, 1971); Sedelle Katz and Mary Ann Mazure, *Understanding the Rape Victim* (New York: Wiley, 1979); C. Kirkpatrick and G. Kanin, "Male Aggression on a University Campus," *American Sociological Review* (1957), 22, pp. 52–58; Paul R. Wilson, *The Other Side of Rape* (St. Lucia, Queensland, Australia: University of Queensland Press, 1978).
6. See MacDonald, *ibid.*; Ann W. Burgess and Linda L. Holmstrom, *Rape: Victims of Crisis* (Bowie, Md.: Brady, 1974); Dukes and Mattley, "Predicting Rape Victim Reportage," *Sociology and Social Research* (1977), 62(1), pp. 63–84.
7. The procedures used to perform the analysis are based on ordinary least squares regression techniques as interpreted by Roberts (1977). It should be emphasized that the analysis is designed to detect a shift in the level of the series before and after the law reform—that is, to answer the question, "Did the sexual assault law have a measurable im-

pact on forcible rape crime statistics?" An equally important question, "What is the nature of the change in crime statistics?" is not addressed by this analysis.

8. Dukes and Mattley (1977), *op. cit.*, p. 68.

9. Department of State Police, Uniform Crime Report for the State of Michigan, 1977.

10. $t = 1.44$, $p < .10$.

11. The increase in convictions as charged was significant at $t = 1.62$, $p < .06$. The findings are consistent with those from a study of California's Robbins Rape Evidence Law (effective January 1975) which restricted evidence on the victim's prior sexual history and of the elimination of jury instruction based on Lord Hale's instruction (effective July of 1975). This study shows that, of all arrests on charges of rape, 9 percent are convicted of the same rape charge before the legal change, 10 percent after the legal change, a statistically significant difference (personal communication, Dr. Mary Demming, Social Science Research Institute, University of Southern California).

12. The interrupted time-series analysis of the crime data indicates that the implementation of the law influenced the rate of convictions as charged. It had a discernible but lesser effect on arrests and little, if any, on reports. To examine how meaningful this relationship was, we imposed a convention that has been used to assess whether or not a particular impact in a social program can be considered "socially significant." See Jacob Cohen, *Statistical Power Analysis for the Behavioral Sciences* (New York: Academic Press, 1969) and Thomas D. Cook, Hilary Appleton, Ross F. Conner, Ann Shafter, Gary Tamkin, and Stephen J. Weber, *"Sesame Street" Revisited* (New York: Russell Sage Foundation, 1975). Specifically, we determined whether the mean difference before and after the intervention was at least one-half the pre-intervention standard deviation after the autocorrelation among observations had been removed. This relationship turns out to be 0.01 for reports, 0.04 for arrests, 0.59 for convictions as charged, and 0.26 for convictions for a lesser charge. Thus, using this standard, the impact of the law on convictions as charged was the only effect that could be considered "socially significant."

13. The reduction in convictions for a lesser offense was statistically significant at $t = -1.40$, $p < .10$. The Demming study, *op. cit.*, in contrast to these findings, found no significant decrease in rape arrests convicted of a lesser charge. This difference may be due to the more extensive changes made in the Michigan statutes, in particular, the substantial redefinition of the crime contained in the degree structure.

14. In order to check the possibility that the significant increase in arrest and conviction rates in Michigan was in fact due to the law and not to more vigorous investigation and prosecution of all serious crimes against the person, time-series analyses were conducted for aggravated assault crimes for the same period. There was not significant relationship of the law reform to these crimes during the period 1972–1978. The statistics were as follows: reports, $t = -0.684$, n.s.; arrests, $t = -0.439$, n.s.; convictions as charged, $t = 0.622$, n.s.

15. Camille LeGrand, "Rape and Rape Laws: Sexism in Society and Law," *California Law Review* (1973), pp. 919–941.

16. National Institute for Law Enforcement and Criminal Justice, LEAA, *Forcible Rape: Final Project Report* (March 1978).

17. Jan BenDor, "Justice After Rape: Legal Reform in Michigan," in Marcia Walker and Stanley Brodsky (eds.), *Sexual Assault: The Victim and the Rapist* (Lexington, Mass.: Lexington Books, 1976), pp. 150–151.

18. National Institute for Law Enforcement and Criminal Justice (1978), *op. cit.*

19. This is an exceptionally high rate when compared with other available statistics. Records from Seattle and Kansas City described in National Institute of Law Enforcement and Criminal Justice, *Forcible Rape: Final Project Report* (1978), show that 45 percent of arrests resulted in convictions. Clearly these data combine with the high conviction rates to reflect the competence of the special investigative unit handling these crimes in the Detroit Police Department and to indicate the ability of Detroit police and prosecutors to identify "winnable" cases in the warrant-issuing process.

20. Personal communication, Mr. Terry Boyle, Chief Prosecutor, Wayne County Prosecutor's Office.

21. The classic study of *The American Jury* by Harry Kalven and Hans Zeisel (Chicago: University of Chicago Press, 1966) indicated a strong tendency for juries to be more lenient than judges in all cases, but particularly in cases of rape.

*Chapter 4*

# THE DYNAMICS OF CHANGE: WHAT CAN A LAW REFORM?

Statistical analysis of the crime data indicates the Michigan law's value in terms of increasing convictions but provides little understanding of the process by which it accomplished change. The dynamics of the change—the interplay between the characteristics of the law and the characteristics of the criminal justice system—are important to explore for at least two reasons. First, other states contemplating or implementing changes in their statutes need to know the success or failure of the Michigan law in terms of its specific provisions. Second, for purposes of understanding law reform as a strategy for social change, other states need to understand the circumstances under which the intentions of the law are met and to identify the optimal conditions for, or barriers to, implementing such a law in terms of the system charged with that task.

In order to provide this information, we systematically sought perspectives on the law, on its implementation in the criminal justice system, and on the resulting changes from a cross section of criminal justice system officials and crisis center staff. These interviews provided insights into the process by which the legal system accommodates efforts at intervention.

41

## Perceptions of Changes in Reports, Arrests, and Convictions

The law reform was comprehensive and complex: It expanded centuries-old definitions of the crime and challenged established assumptions that guided the investigation and conduct of a case. Because the law dealt with rape, a crime that has always received unique treatment in the system, we expected case processing for this crime to be especially resistant to change. Instead, we found that the law's success was a measure of the system's response to an "idea whose time has come." Importantly, many provisions of the law were compatible with the interests of participants in the system. While not necessarily responsive to all the concerns and the attitudes of the participants, the law functioned to provide certain incentives to these participants that enhanced their willingness to implement it.

The law reform effort was in part a response to an increase in rape reports, but neither the crime statistics nor the responses of those interviewed indicate that the law had much effect on reports. But reporting rates are exceptional in this respect. Most respondents believe that the law has meant a shift in the balance of power between the complainant and the defendant. And, consistent with the Task Force's goals, crime statistics show that the law, in fact, has improved the chances of conviction by reducing the significance of some factors relevant to the crime. In this regard, particularly by prohibiting the use of sex past information, it has also improved the victim's experience with the system. Different types of victims now successfully prosecute, for the law has expanded the legal coverage given (including the sanctions that are imposed) to certain kinds of cases. Apparently, the law has done so without jeopardizing defendants' rights. According to respondents, all this has been accomplished in part because of the comprehensiveness of the new law.

### Reports

Respondents believe that the increase in reported rapes results from enlightened attitudes that encourage victims to come forward. Law reform and absolute increases in violent crime play a role, they said, but as shown in Table 4–1, they most commonly

Table 4–1    Reasons for Increase in Reports of Rape (N = 165)

| *Reasons Reported as among the Three Most Important* | *Percentage of Respondents Citing Each* |
| --- | --- |
| Change in public attitudes toward rape | 73.8 |
| Effects of the women's liberation movement | 45.2 |
| Increased sensitivity of the criminal justice system | 41.7 |
| Effects of the new CSC law | 39.3 |
| General increase in violence | 34.5 |
| Sexual permissiveness | 16.1 |
| Increased convictions | 8.9 |
| Influence of pornography | 7.1 |

NOTE: Because respondents were allowed multiple responses to this question, total responses exceed 100 percent.

cited change in public attitudes toward rape, followed by the influence of the women's movement and increased sensitivity on the part of the criminal justice system as reasons for the increase in reports. As a group, defense attorneys were alone in asserting that "sexual permissiveness" was among the five most important influences on reporting rates. Their view is consistent with their role as advocates, implying as it does that the defendant is not culpable if the sexual assault was encouraged by a woman's permissiveness. Generally, respondents said that reporting trends reflect not the incidence of the crime but a greater willingness to report it.[1] This perspective is supported by their perception of an increase in certain kinds of cases. As discussed later, respondents perceive sharply accelerating reports of incest cases and rapes of male victims. These cases can be especially traumatic for victims to report. Respondents also observe more "marginal" cases, including sexual assaults involving women alleged to be prostitutes. Consistent with the time-series analyses, less than half the respondents credited the law with the dramatic rise in rape reports. Respondents do view it as contributing to these trends, but believe that changing norms in society and within their own professional spheres make the critical difference.[2]

## Convictions

One of the law reformers' goals was to increase conviction rates, a concern shared by members of the criminal justice system. The time-series analyses demonstrated an increase in convictions related to the law, and the views of a majority of our respondents confirmed the relationship. Nearly three-fourths of those interviewed thought that prosecutors' chances of winning sexual assault cases had improved.

As shown in Table 4–2, crisis center staff were unanimous in their assertion that prosecutors' chances for winning cases had improved. Their assessment seems to reflect their enthusiasm for the law in general and for its increased protection for victims in particular. In addition, police and defense attorneys, who should be especially sensitive to the issue, overwhelmingly agreed that prosecutors' chances for conviction had improved, while judges and prosecutors themselves were more reserved in assessing the change.

## Impact of Specific Provisions on Convictions

Unlike reporting rates, which seem unrelated to the law, improving conviction rates are linked by respondents to specific features of the law that minimize discretion. Nearly half of them said that the law's prohibition of sexual history evidence was responsible for improving chances of winning CSC cases (see Table 4–3). The degree structure was cited by 26 percent of the respondents, and 17 percent said that the improvement was brought about by elimination of the need to prove resistance and nonconsent.

Some respondents thought that factors other than the law were responsible for improving prosecutors' chances for convictions. Change in public attitudes toward both women and rape victims were cited as contributing factors; and some cited changes in the attitudes of members of the criminal justice system. A few re-

**Table 4–2   Percentage of Respondents Reporting Change in Prosecutors' Chances of Winning (N = 157)**

| Actors | Greatly Improved | Improved | Same | Diminished | Greatly Diminished |
|---|---|---|---|---|---|
| Judges | 18.8 | 50.0 | 28.1 | 3.1 | 0 |
| Prosecutors | 10.0 | 67.5 | 17.5 | 8.0 | 0 |
| Defense Attorneys | 40.7 | 40.0 | 6.7 | 3.3 | 3.3 |
| Police | 16.7 | 69.4 | 13.9 | 0 | 0 |
| Crisis Center Staff | 26.3 | 73.7 | 0 | 0 | 0 |
| Total | 22.3 | 59.9 | 14.6 | 2.5 | .6 |

Table 4–3    Reasons for Prosecutors' Improved Chances of Winning (N = 157)

| Type of Change | Percentage of Respondents Mentioning Change |
|---|---|
| Changes in statute | |
| (1) Restrictions on past sexual history evidence | 44.1 |
| (2) Degree structure | 25.8 |
| (3) Changes in resistance and consent standards | 17.0 |
| (4) Unspecified statute changes | 11.7 |
| (5) Codification and clarification of terminology | 7.6 |
| Changes in society | 11.7 |
| Changes in the criminal justice system | 7.6 |
| Changes in types of cases | 3.5 |

NOTE: Because respondents were allowed up to three different answers to this question, total responses exceed 100 percent.

spondents considered the inclusion of more marginal cases an advantage for prosecutors, contrary to the initial fears of prosecutors who believed that these marginal cases would be more difficult to try and would result in a reduced conviction rate.[3] Those who did not believe that prosecutors' chances of winning have improved (26 percent of respondents) reasoned that the law was too complicated (adversely affecting charging, plea-bargaining, or case presentation) or that a complainant's demeanor is still crucial to a case despite the law reform. Generally, there appears to be consensus among respondents that the CSC statute increased the "winnability" of sexual assault cases. And because respondents believe that specific provisions of the law are crucial to that change, it would appear that, even in the absence of vast social change, the law itself can exert some influence to improve the chances of conviction.

## Plea-Bargaining

Plea-bargaining is an essential tool in the criminal justice system in that it reduces the time and resources required for each case. The majority of criminal cases are resolved through this mechanism. When used in criminal sexual conduct cases, plea-bargaining has the additional advantage of sparing the victim the prolonged and often painful trial experience. Concern about plea-bargaining derives from fear that it will promote lower charges and lighter sentences.

Architects of the law anticipated this possibility. The plea-bargaining process was a major consideration when the degree structure was incorporated into the law. The four degrees of criminal sexual conduct—a "staircasing" approach—were in part designed to assure that defendants will plea to a lower sex offense rather than to a crime such as assault and battery. By specifying degrees of criminal sexual conduct, they limited charge reductions to sex-related offenses. Because there is mandatory minimum sentence for second sex offenses, a defendant convicted twice of sexual assault theoretically faces certain imprisonment.

There are two ways in which defendants can bargain with their guilty pleas. In one, they agree to plead guilty on the condition that the prosecutor agrees to reduce the charge. In this situation, for example, an individual charged with CSC in the first degree might plead guilty to CSC in the third degree, thereby lowering the maximum amount of possible punishment. The plea is entered before the judge by the defense during pre-trial procedures or at trial. In the second type of plea, which is a somewhat controversial practice, the accused agrees to plead guilty if the judge will agree to a specified maximum sentence. The judge should consult with the prosecutor for his or her view of the case before agreeing to a negotiated sentence, but often may not. It is also true that the defendant can bargain for both a reduced charge and a negotiated sentence, with the prosecutor agreeing to reduce the charge and the judge agreeing to limit the sentence.

Because the CSC statute is more complicated than the typical carnal knowledge rape statute, there was concern that attorneys' confusion would encourage plea-bargaining, thereby pushing more cases through the informal system and leading to low charges and fewer or lighter sentences. And if more cases were plea-bargained, there would be more opportunity to thwart the intent of the law, especially with regard to admission of information about a victim's previous sexual activities. On the other hand, the relative anonymity and speedy case conclusion resulting from plea-bargaining offer the possibility of reduced trauma for the victim. Also, defendants may prefer plea-bargaining to avoid the publicity of court trial and the stigma attached to the crime.

The responses of judges, prosecutors, and defense attorneys, when asked about the frequency of reduced charges and negotiated sentence plea-bargaining in criminal sexual conduct cases, corroborated the findings from the crime statistics. Although individual responses ranged broadly among all actors, within actor groups, and within counties, their differences were not statistically significant. Approximately half of those questioned indicated that most sexual assault cases were resolved by plea-bargaining. Reduced-charge plea-bargains were reported to be more frequent than negotiated sentences. When asked to compare the rate of plea-bargaining in sexual assault cases with the rates for equally serious crimes, most respondents (59 percent) said they were about the same.

Those who believed there was more plea-bargaining in sexual assault cases (28 percent) provided explanations related to (1) the impact of trial on the victim or the defendant, (2) plea-bargaining policies within the prosecutor's office, or (3) characteristics of the new CSC law. One Detroit defense attorney described how he increases plea-bargaining by capitalizing on the stress involved in pursuing a case:

> *Part of the defense attorney's job it to get complainants tired of cases. Due to the dramatic nature of the crime, prosecutors and complainants may want to settle (plea-bargain) more in these cases. Victims probably say, "Go ahead (and accept a reduced charge). I don't want to come to court anymore."*

Other respondents explained that increased plea-bargaining in CSC cases resulted from office policies discouraging plea-bargaining in other crimes; the resulting system overload was then reduced by bargaining in CSC cases. Several attributed an increase to the options for pleas provided by the degree structure. Few who perceived *more* plea-bargaining in CSC cases mentioned the difficulty of successfully prosecuting in court.

Indeed, those who detected *less* plea-bargaining in sexual assault cases (13 percent) attributed it to (1) the relative ease with which sexual assault defendants can win a trial, followed by (2) a prosecutor's office policy discouraging plea-bargaining in CSC cases, (3) the stigma attached to the crime, deterring defendants' admission of guilt, and (4) the brutal or serious nature of the offense, which makes prosecutors reluctant to plea-bargain.

Among the counties studied there were some differences in reported rates of reduced-charge plea-bargaining. These appear to be explained largely by policies of the prosecutors' offices which either encourage or restrict plea-bargaining in sexual assault cases. In some jurisdictions, it may be encouraged to reduce case load or to minimize victim trauma. In others, policies discouraging plea-bargaining are typically the result of a chief prosecutor's strong "law and order" stance. Several respondents said the increased attention activists have given to sexual assault cases also had led to policies limiting plea-bargaining.

Some respondents feel the stigma attached to a CSC conviction leads to increased plea-bargaining, while some believe it reduces plea-bargaining. Both observations have merit: Some defendants may plead guilty to avoid a public trial that would reveal the details of the assault, while others refuse to plead guilty because they do not want to admit they committed a sexual assault.

We specifically asked respondents whether they thought the CSC law had produced changes in plea-bargaining, and a majority (59 percent) indicated that there had been none. Among those who believed there is less plea-bargaining now, changes in office policy rather than in the law were most often cited for the decrease (50 percent of responses). Over two-thirds (68 percent) of those who thought that plea-bargaining had increased under the CSC statute credit the law's degree structure with the change. Some claimed that this feature of the law provides more reasonable options for bargaining, a result that is consistent with the goals of those who drafted the law.

Given the institutional reliance on plea-bargaining, the degree structure would seem to enhance an important component of the bureaucracy's functioning. But the general consensus that the frequency of plea-bargaining has not changed may be interpreted in several ways. First, these data refute earlier claims that the law's complexity would force more cases into this avenue of case resolution where the rules of evidence do not always apply. A similar interpretation is that since the law has proved flexible in meeting the bureaucratic demand for plea-bargaining, attorneys are likely to respond positively and to make good use of its other features.

Alternatively, respondents' estimates that plea-bargaining remains at previous levels may be disheartening to critics of the criminal justice system who have advocated a greater reliance on plea-bargaining to reduce victim trauma. When a case reaches the courtroom, conviction is uncertain, and the victim of sexual assault must publicly give testimony on the witness stand.

Finally, the stability of plea-bargaining as an entrenched feature of the criminal justice process is a disappointment to those who had hoped its frequency would lessen. Virtually all rape crisis counselors indicated that they were unhappy with the pleas in at least a third of the cases they handled. They gave a number of reasons for their dissatisfaction, most often mentioning prosecutors' failure to consult victims in this regard and, according to one counselor, the victims' subsequent feeling that "their efforts to prosecute have not been meaningful." Another said that "victims are upset (by plea-bargaining) because they don't feel the defendant has been punished or because they fear retaliation." Other counselors described specific cases in which they felt plea-bargaining had been inappropriate given the "grisly" nature of the crime. In summarizing her feelings about plea bargaining, one Detroit counselor said, "Even when the defendant has a past record, the crime is viewed as trivial. And the cost of a trial is large."

Overall, the finding that plea-bargaining continues at previous rates speaks to the tenacity of institutional traditions. Given the importance of plea-bargaining in the system, the law reformers could not hope to eliminate it. Instead, by incorporating a degree structure into the statute, they could exert more control over a process whose continuation was assured by the dictates of the bureaucracy.

## Perceptions of Changes in Courtroom Procedures

As with any crime, the successful prosecution of a rape case involves the presentation of an array of evidence and events to persuade judges and juries that the defendant actually committed the offense. Law sets the stage for the conduct of the case by defining evidentiary requirements. The role of each actor, however, is defined by convention and informal norms, and is only minimally influenced by legal strictures. To fully explore the process by which CSC convictions are achieved, we examined changes in evidence requirements as well as courtroom tactics, juries' behavior, and judges' discretion to determine how they complemented, contributed to, or confounded the law's impact.

## Evidence and Circumstances Related to Conviction

In a CSC case, determination of the guilt or innocence of the defendant rests on evidence specific to the crime as well as on conventions that guide the system in any trial. Some of the factors that are weighed relate to evidence of circumstances surrounding the assault: defendant's use of a weapon; penetration; physical injury to complainant; nonconsent of complainant; resistance of complainant; outcry by complainant; corroborating witnesses. Others relate to events after the assault: flight by the accused; prompt report by the complainant; thorough police investigation; and accurate collection of laboratory evidence. Still others concern characteristics of the trial: whether the defendant takes the stand or not, and his demeanor if he does; and the complainant's demeanor when she takes the stand. Finally, the outcome may be influenced by evidence of behavior that predates the assault, such as the defendant's criminal record and the victim's sexual history. In rape cases, legal tradition and social attitudes have always made the victim of the crime the focus of the case.

We expected that many of these items would be less important to the prosecution's case under the criminal sexual conduct law than they had been to prosecutions under old rape statutes. Penetration, for example, is no longer a necessary element of the offense (CSC in the second and fourth degrees requires only "sexual contact," not penetration). Nonetheless, some prosecutors did indicate that CSC cases involving penetration were easier to win.

We identified eleven items (including penetration) which were known to have been important to successful prosecutions under the prior rape law but which, we hypothesized, now would be less important. Some items were specifically addressed by the reformed law. The complainant's sexual history is generally excluded (section 520j); resistance by complainant is no longer required (section 520i); and corroborating witnesses are not needed (section 520h). Outcry by complainant at time of the assault was expected to be less important because it amounts only to evidence of resistance, and the law's focus was also expected to diminish the importance of nonconsent. The law was designed so that proof of the defendant's use of a weapon and physical injury to complainant would not be as critical to the success of the prosecutor's case under the new statute.

The law reformers hoped that the general effects of the law, along with changes in society's attitudes toward women and rape, would generally create more trust of complainants, and that these changes would thus diminish the importance of other aspects of the prosecutor's case. With the credibility of sexual assault complainants less open to question, prompt report by the complainant and her demeanor at trial might decrease in importance.

We asked judges, prosecutors, and defense attorneys to rate each item's importance to the prosecution of a criminal sexual conduct case in the first degree (CSC1). The respondents were then asked to rate how important each item had been to the prosecution of an equivalent case under the old statutes.

As indicated in Table 4–4, the perceived importance of all eleven items decreased under the reformed law. But while all eleven items were viewed as having decreased in importance, all are still considered important—or at least useful—to the prosecution of a CSC1 case. Nonconsent of the complainant and the victim's demeanor at trial were rated as the two most important items

Table 4–4   Change in Importance of Items to Successful Prosecutions— Mean Scores[1] (Respondents: Judges, Prosecutors, Defense Attorneys) (N = 71)

| Item | Mean Importance Under Reformed Law | Mean Importance Under Old Law |
|---|---|---|
| Complainant's sexual history | 4.74[11] | 2.66[7] |
| Resistance of complainant | 3.25[8] | 2.11[3] |
| Outcry by complainant | 4.21[10] | 3.36[11] |
| Corroborating witness | 3.73[9] | 3.19[10] |
| Laboratory evidence | 3.04[7] | 2.74[8] |
| Nonconsent of complainant | 1.97[1] | 1.47[1] |
| Physical injury to complainant | 2.77[5] | 2.50[6] |
| Defendant's use of a weapon | 3.02[6] | 2.84[9] |
| Prompt report by complainant | 2.56[4] | 2.43[5] |
| Thorough police investigation | 2.47[3] | 2.40[4] |
| Complainant's demeanor at trial | 2.02[2] | 1.97[2] |

[1] Based on a scale of 1 = "Absolutely Essential" to 7 = "Useless." Superscripts represent rank order.

under both the old and the new laws. Nonconsent remains the most important, despite the fact that it registered a notable decrease in value as an element of the prosecutor's proofs. The continuing influence of these two items indicates that victim characteristics remain an important consideration, but apparently the victim's sexual history does not. Seven of the items showed a statistically significant decrease in perceived importance, the most striking of which was the reduction in importance attributed to the complainant's sexual history. Table 4–4 shows its perceived significance decreased by a substantial margin. The complainant's sexual history is now viewed as the least important of the tested items, but the respondents said that it still helps the prosecutor's case if the victim's background is unimpeachable.

Resistance by complainant and the closely related item, outcry by complainant, also registered significant decreases. Respondents also noted that the importance of corroborating witnesses had decreased. The diminished value of these four items is a direct reflection of the three specific provisions of the law noted above —namely, exclusion of complainant's sexual history, elimination of the resistance requirement (which encompasses evidence of outcry), and elimination of the need for corroborating witnesses.

The law therefore appears to have exerted control over the influence of specific evidence, particularly that of sexual history. But consent and character remain critical issues. As one prosecutor put it, "You can't legislate a credible rape victim."

## Courtroom Tactics

Although the CSC statute has altered the evidentiary requirements, it appears that the routine, day-to-day functions of the system are not much affected. Procedural changes notwithstanding, defense attorneys and prosecutors said that in general they had not changed their courtroom tactics. Like the law's relatively benign effect on plea-bargaining observed by respondents, this may have favored the law's implementation. It increased convictions but required minimal effort to be incorporated into the system's basic operating procedures.

Table 4–5 shows that only one-quarter of prosecutors and less than one-half of defense attorneys said that they had changed their courtroom tactics. Among judges, who are perhaps the more

Table 4–5   Changes in Courtroom Tactics of Prosecutors and Defense Attorneys

| Actors | Percentage of Respondents | | | |
| --- | --- | --- | --- | --- |
| | Perceived Changes in Prosecutors | | Perceived Changes in Defense Attorneys | |
| | Yes | No | Yes | No |
| Judges (N = 33) | 42.4 | 57.6 | 45.5 | 54.5 |
| Prosecutors (N = 32) | 21.9 | 78.1 | — | — |
| Defense Attorneys (N = 26) | — | — | 46.2 | 53.8 |
| Total (N = 59) | 32.3 | 67.7 | 45.8 | 54.2 |

impartial reporters of the process, a majority (58 percent) noted no change in the advocates' approach to trials.[4]

Prosecutors who said that they had changed their practices gave a number of explanations. Several said they present the case to jurors differently—that is, they worry less about proving the victim's "worthiness" and can concentrate on showing that the criminal act occurred. Similarly, others said the restrictions on evidence of a victim's sexual history meant they no longer must build a case to excuse or justify a victim's sexual past. They also mentioned the changes in the corroboration and resistance requirements and the new law's degree structure. Without the need to produce witnesses or to prove resistance, prosecutors have fewer elements to establish. Those few judges who detected a different approach in the prosecution also noted changes in treatment and selection of jurors, and a shift in emphasis brought about by the exclusion of sexual history evidence. Like prosecutors, several judges also noted the influence of the degree structure.

Those who expected massive revisions in the way sexual assault cases are handled may be disappointed by the fact that so few prosecutors have sensed a need to change tactics. But since most cases are settled through plea-bargaining, changes in courtroom tactics involve a small proportion of all cases prosecuted. From another viewpoint, the fact that tactical changes have been minor reflects positively on the new statute. Prior to its passage by the Michigan legislature, a number of influential prosecutors opposed the law. They feared that the degree structure would impede their ability to plea-bargain, and that the term "sexual assault," because it lacked the impact of the word "rape," would reduce conviction rates while adding unnecessary complexity to case processing. The absence of these difficulties in the Michigan experience should allay the fears of prosecutors in states considering similar reforms. As discussed elsewhere, a majority of prosecutors feel that their chances of winning sexual assault cases have improved under the new law—improved, these data would indicate, with a minimum change of strategy on the part of prosecutors. As one prosecutor summarized it, "The law's value is essentially symbolic. It hasn't produced dramatic courtroom changes, but is a catalyst for change in attitudes."

Much of the law's effectiveness depends upon the elimination of defense strategies designed to "rake women over the coals," as one defense attorney described it. The exclusion of sexual history evidence and the elimination of corroboration and resistance from the prosecutor's proofs should markedly alter the classic defense in sexual assault cases. But less than half of defense attorneys stated that they had changed their tactics. Among those who had, defense attorneys said they had changed their cross-examination of the victim and general approach to the defense mainly because of the restriction on sexual history evidence. And as a defense attorney put it, "Over the last five or ten years, Detroit has changed. You just can't win by showing that the victim wasn't wearing underwear."

According to another defense attorney:

> *Though I'm embarrassed to admit it, I used to bring the woman's character in all the time. If I was successful in convincing the jury that she was a "loose woman who gave it away on every street corner," they'd disbelieve her, even in a stranger rape. (Sex past) always mattered, even in a brutal rape. You could hint to the jury that she invited the attack.*

Some defense attorneys also reported that the new law's degree structure had prompted them to change their tactics by forcing them to present their evidence more methodically. Several indicated, too, that the law's complexity forces them to spend extra time explaining it to jurors. Judges generally agreed with the majority of defense attorneys that changes in defense strategies were primarily due to the exclusion of sexual history evidence.

One judge who felt that defense attorneys had not changed explained his reasons as follows:

> *The victim was always treated better than people believed. Here in B county, we treat the victim with courtesy and taste, and al-*

*ways did. A good trial lawyer knew it was crazy to go into her sex past—only crude, dumb ones did. He can still use those tactics, but it's stupid because it alienates the jury. There are so many ways to prove someone's lying that it's absurd to go into prior sex record.*

### Defense Attorney Investigation of a Victim

A number of defense attorneys said that, despite the law, they are able to introduce testimony about a woman's sexual history, and three-quarters of those we interviewed said that during their case preparation they actively seek this sort of information about a complainant. In their pre-trial investigations, two-thirds indicated that they also seek information related to the complainant's credibility, character, and general reputation (including whether the complainant has a criminal record, a history of reporting sexual assaults, or a psychiatric history). One defense attorney gave this explanation for his investigative practices: "People don't fantasize about being robbed, but some fantasize about being raped." Overall about two-thirds (62 percent) of the defense attorneys said that they had not changed their inquiries about a complainant under the CSC statutes. Among those who had, eight out of ten now simply put less emphasis on learning about the complainant's sexual history.

Changes in the law and in public attitudes notwithstanding, some juries and judges may still accept the idea that the victim was a promiscuous woman who somehow enticed or lured the defendant into raping her. In their investigative practices, the majority of defense attorneys seem to anticipate the opportunity to take advantage of these continuing biases. One defense attorney said, "Now you just discredit the victim with kid gloves." Apparently, these data indicate, the law has limited the defense attorneys' prerogative to impeach the victim's character, but has not eliminated it altogether.

A few defense attorneys refuse to take sexual assault cases as a matter of policy. According to one,

*There is no political rationale for defending them. It's an oppressive and discriminatory offense. When representing a client you must defend him or her to the best of your ability. In a sexual assault case that would mean appealing to certain sexist attitudes and contributing to very bad sterotypical patterns in society.*

The same lawyer has brought civil suits on behalf of rape victims who were unhappy with the way the criminal justice system had handled their cases. Two attorneys defend clients accused of sexual assault only when the defense theory is identification, not consent. Said one, "I do not feel that a woman's sexual history is ever relevant in a rape case."

## Jury Behavior

Even for victims of the stereotypical rape (a brutal attack by a stranger) juries have been unsympathetic unless the victim is above reproach.[5] To ascertain, if only in a cursory manner, whether changes in jury behavior might have confounded some of the apparent impact of the CSC law, we asked judges about jury behavior under the new law. Sixty percent of the judges thought jury behavior had changed; the others thought it had not.

Seven out of eight who observed a change believed that jurors were now more likely to convict in sexual assault cases. But most were quick to say that the willingness to convict is *not* a by-product of the law. Rather, they most often cited (1) changes in public attitudes regarding sexual behavior, (2) public awareness about rape, and (3) the impact of the women's movement as reasons for the change.

According to those who credit jurors with a more enlightened view of rape and its victims, it would appear that the women's movement has legitimized the concerns of women in general and of rape victims in particular. In this vein a number of judges expanded on their observation that jurors were more likely to convict. In the opinion of one,

> *Jurors are more liberal in their sexual attitudes than they were three years ago, but they do not reflect the same attitude as that in the CSC statute—they are still fairly conservative regarding women and sexuality. For example, you can get a conviction for a hitch-hiking rape, but you still cannot get a conviction in cases involving a pregnant complainant or a prostitute.*

A judge who said that jury behavior had not changed illuminated the obstacles to justice for rape victims—and the task ahead for anti-rape activists—when he stated:

> *Education is the essential factor. There is some reason [why] people don't want to convict on rape complaints, but I don't have an*

*explanation for it. Down deep, people feel there is some reason why women are raped. Men believe women can't be raped. And I don't find women sympathetic or understanding toward victims. There seems to be a general social feeling against victims of rape.*

## Judicial Discretion

With the evidentiary provision prohibiting the use of prior sexual history information, Michigan's statute swept away a long tradition of revictimization in the courtroom. It severely restricts the introduction of sexual history evidence to a few circumstances. Only evidence of the victim's past sexual conduct with the defendant and evidence of specific instances of sexual activity showing the source or origin of semen, pregnancy, or disease are admissible. Furthermore, if the defendant proposes to offer such evidence at trial, the defense attorney must file a written motion and offer of proof within ten days after arraignment. The judge may then order an *in-camera* hearing to determine whether the proposed evidence is admissible. If information discovered during the course of trial indicates that certain sexual history evidence may be admissible under one of the exceptions to the exclusionary rule, the judge may order an *in-camera* hearing to determine admissibility.

We asked respondents how often such hearings take place, and most (two-thirds) said they were rarely or never held. When *in-camera* hearings are held, consistent with the law, they most commonly focus on whether sexual history evidence is admissible or they are requested because the victim is a juvenile. We are unable to determine why *in-camera* hearings are so infrequent. Perhaps questions about the admissibility of evidence rarely arise. It is also possible that the time-consuming nature of these hearings discourages application of this provision of the law. In the experience of one prosecutor, the outcome of *in-camera* hearing is predictable: "Judges favor the defense in their rulings. In a close call the defendant wins—and the victim loses."

A number of judges clearly welcomed the exclusion of sexual history evidence. One noted that, while he had rarely admitted this evidence in the past, the new law "gives us something to hang our hats on." Nevertheless, there continues to be concern that judges will admit prior sexual history evidence beyond the narrow exceptions. At trial, the defense may still try to cross-

Table 4–6   **Extent to Which Judge's Discretion Can Control the Outcome of a CSC Jury Trial**

|  | Percentage of Respondents | | | | |
|---|---|---|---|---|---|
| *Amount of Control* | *Judges (N = 31)* | *Prosecutors (N = 40)* | *Defense Attorneys (N = 29)* | *Crisis Center Staff (N = 14)* | *Total (N = 114)* |
| Completely | 4.2 | 0 | 10.3 | 14.3 | 5.3 |
| A great deal | 25.8 | 62.5 | 62.1 | 50.0 | 50.9 |
| Somewhat | 9.7 | 30.0 | 24.1 | 35.7 | 23.9 |
| Very little | 41.9 | 5.0 | 3.4 | 0 | 14.0 |
| Not at all | 19.4 | 2.5 | 0 | 0 | 6.1 |

examine a victim about her sexual past. Judges may rule out such questions, but the prosecutors usually must object on their own initiative. In any instance, the judge can decide where to limit the inquiry; the judge's discretion before and during trial is the critical factor. The CSC statute specifically sought to eliminate judicial discretion in this regard by acknowledging that when they exercise their considerable power, it is often to the detriment of rape victims. To determine whether the new law was in fact exerting more control over judges' decision making, we asked respondents several questions about judicial discretion.

First, we asked judges, prosecutors, defense attorneys, and rape crisis center personnel about the degree to which a judge's discretionary behavior could control the outcome of a jury trial. Not surprisingly, there was disagreement. Judges professed to have far less power than other respondents attributed to them. The data displayed in Table 4–6 indicate that, although 61 percent of judges said they could control the outcome of CSC jury trials "very little" or "not at all," 93 percent of prosecutors, 97 percent of defense attorneys, and all the rape crisis center staff members felt that judges had a considerable degree of control over the outcome.

Second, we asked about the ways in which judges can affect the outcome of jury trials. The responses are presented in rank order: (1) by ruling on the admissibility of evidence, especially evidence related to a victim's sexual history; (2) by persuading and leading jurors through their demeanor and other subtle behavior; and (3) by ruling on motions and instructions to juries. For instance, one defense attorney recounted a case under the new law in which he requested the judge to instruct the jury that consent was implied because the victim did not scream when she was attacked. The judge granted the request. Jury instructions seem particularly vulnerable to abuse. In the words of one prosecutor, "Judges can always shaft you on jury instructions. They can ignore the law and instruct in a way that's favorable to the defendant and for which the prosecution has no appeal."

But the influence of judges' demeanor or other subtle behavior is the most troublesome of their discretionary powers. There are numerous opportunities for judges to sway a jury by tone of voice, facial expressions, or a line of questioning, and of course, these nuances rarely appear in the record of the trial. The ideal role of the judge is to remain neutral and unmoved by trials, but in practice their biases may exert considerable influence. At least one-third of all groups (except judges) named demeanor as a way judges control trials. Only one in seven judges mentioned it.

Despite the importance they attach to judicial discretion, only 40 percent of prosecutors and defense attorneys could identify a case where it actually changed what otherwise would have been the outcome of the trial. The majority of these involved rulings on the admissibility of evidence, especially evidence related to a victim's sexual history. There were also several cases in which a respondent believed the judge's demeanor had changed the outcome.

Table 4–7 indicates that nearly three-quarters of all respondents believe that the new law has changed the amount of discretion a judge has in a CSC case. And a clear majority of respondents (69 percent) thought the restriction of sexual history evidence was responsible for the change.

Table 4–7    Changes in Judges' Discretion, Resulting from the New CSC Law

| Actors | Percentage of Respondents | |
|---|---|---|
| | Change | No Change |
| Judges (N = 33) | 60.6 | 39.4 |
| Prosecutors (N = 36) | 69.4 | 30.6 |
| Defense Attorneys (N = 28) | 89.3 | 10.7 |
| Crisis Center Staff (N = 8) | 87.5 | 12.5 |
| Total (N = 105) | 73.3 | 26.7 |

Table 4–8    Frequency with Which Judges Allow Sex History Evidence as
             Reported by Defense Attorneys and Crisis Center Staff

|  | Percentage of Respondents | | |
| Frequency | Defense Attorneys (N = 22) | Crisis Center Staff (N = 12) | Total (N = 34) |
|---|---|---|---|
| Frequently | 22.7 | 8.3 | 17.6 |
| Sometimes | 22.7 | 33.3 | 26.5 |
| Rarely | 45.5 | 50.0 | 47.1 |
| Never | 9.1 | 8.3 | 8.8 |

Consistent with the data on the use of *in-camera* hearings, nearly two-thirds of judges indicated that they "seldom" had to rule on the admissibility of evidence of a CSC complainant's sex past, and the same percentage said they never allowed it to be introduced. But other respondents estimated that judges admitted such evidence more often. As shown in Table 4–8, nearly half of the defense attorneys and rape crisis center staff said that judges allow this testimony "sometimes" or "frequently." Only three of twenty-two defense attorneys said judges "never" admit such evidence.

Because of the importance of sexual past information, we attempted to determine the circumstances under which it was allowed to be introduced at trial. The judges said they allow questioning about a complainant's sexual history when (1) the complainant has a history of consensual sexual relations with the defendant, (2) there is a question of consent, and (3) the complaining witness commits perjury regarding her sexual history or practices. Some judges also said they allow this evidence when a complainant has a psychiatric history, a criminal record, a history of making rape reports, or when she is a prostitute.

Defense attorneys and crisis center staff were also asked to describe the circumstances under which judges admit sexual history evidence. The most frequent response (from 56 percent of respondents) was that (1) this testimony is allowed when the complaining witness previously had a consensual sexual relationship with the defendant. Also commonly reported, consistent with the judges' responses, were instances in which (2) the complainant is a prostitute, (3) there is a question of consent, (4) the complainant commits perjury, and (5) if the prosecutor claims the complainant is a virgin. Sexual history information may *properly* be admitted when the defendant and complainant have a previous sexual relationship.

Some attorneys also argue that frequent unsubstantiated reports of sexual assault or a psychiatric history indicating a pattern of imagined rapes, for example, justify admitting sexual history evidence. Others claim that a defendant should be able to offer evidence that a complainant is a prostitute, if the defense is that she falsely charged sexual assault in order to extract payment. But these circumstances clearly fall outside the law's restrictions; the responses suggest that judges may sometimes fail to observe the prohibition on sexual history evidence.

One judge said that he had always ruled out such evidence because he takes a "strong view of rape—it is a terrible and heinous crime and no woman who is raped should suffer any more than she already has." But he continued:

> *What does sex past have to do with a case unless she's a prostitute? Or if she's out hitchhiking with a short skirt and no bra, she asked for it and I'll admit [that evidence]. That isn't past sexual history information and therefore it's not restricted.*

Another judge presented a more enlightened view. He said that when faced with the decision to admit sexual history,

> *You've got to play it by ear. There'd have to be some damn good reasons [to admit it]. I'd be very reluctant to allow people to get into somebody's personal situation. In the past there were so many theatrics and degrading of complainants with reputation stuff. We used to have to let that go and the complainant would be miserable. It's much more civilized now.*

The occasional but continuing improper use of sexual history evidence would seem to reflect biases that are pervasive despite the legislative attempt to hamper judicial discretion. The exercise of that discretion to admit sexual history information when it is inappropriate means that victims cannot be assured of immunity from "rape in the courtroom," and qualifies the more general belief among respondents that both victims and prosecutors can expect improved experiences in the courtroom.

Respondents in one county repeatedly mentioned a judge who is infamous for his stated belief that "no woman can be raped against her will." This judge routinely allows cross-examination regarding the complainant's sexual history. For the victim who has the misfortune to have her case assigned to that judge, the law reform offers little. And unlike the defendant, the victim has no chance to appeal.

## Influence of Specific Provisions on Overall Impact of the Law

From the respondents' point of view, the most important effects of the law revolve around the revisions in evidence requirements and the clarity of the degree structure in charging, plea-bargaining, prosecution, and sentencing. These components of the law for the most part reduce the confusion inherent in case processing and contribute to improvement in conviction rates. But the feature of the law most often credited with improving victim experience is also seen by respondents as its most important contribution overall. Two-thirds named the prohibition of sex past information as the most significant aspect of the law, underscoring its generally pervasive influence.

Table 4–9 also shows that half the respondents felt the degree structure was an important aspect of the law, noting specifically the changes in elements of the crime that comprise the prosecutor's proofs and their effect on charging and plea-bargaining

Table 4–9    Three Most Significant Aspects of Michigan's Criminal Sexual Conduct Statute (N = 160)

| Type of Change Reported as Among Three Most Significant | Percentage of Respondents Mentioning Change |
|---|---|
| Restriction of sexual history evidence | 68.1 |
| Degree structure | 49.4 |
| Codification of statutes and revision in terminology | 31.9 |
| Impact on society | 22.5 |
| Removal of resistance standards | 16.9 |
| Gender neutral | 14.4 |
| Criminal justice system handling of crime | 14.4 |
| Age of victim in statutory rape | 11.8 |
| Victim experience in criminal justice system | 10.6 |
| Ability to charge separated spouse | 5.6 |

NOTE: Because multiple responses to this question were allowed, total responses exceed 100 percent.

decisions. Several of these respondents mentioned that, under the new statute, penetration is not required and contact alone constitutes an offense. Nearly a third of all respondents (32 percent) discussed the revision in terminology or codification of old statutes; most felt that the increased specificity of definitions was helpful.

Some respondents believe that alterations in resistance and consent standards are important. They also noted the law's expanded coverage for separated spouses, incest victims, and males, and its lowered age of consent. Several referred to *in-camera* hearings and to changes in corroboration requirements.

Nearly a quarter of respondents mentioned effects of the law that could be termed symbolic: public awareness of the crime, reporting increases, and the fact that the law treats rape like other assaultive crimes. Most of those who mentioned these effects felt they had been salutory, but two respondents felt that the publicity surrounding the law's passage had encouraged false reporting and had led to more unfounded complaints of sexual assault.

Some respondents mentioned improvements in victim experience without linking these to specific aspects of the law. They believe that the new law is more humane—that there is less "rape in the courtroom"—or that it offers the possibility of successful prosecution to groups such as prostitutes or women who know their attackers. Except for these observations, few people discussed those facets of the law that most challenge traditional assumptions about culturally acceptable behavior towards women. Although some respondents did mention that the degree structure now includes "contact" as an offense (that is, CSC2 and CSC4), they were likely to do so in the context of prosecutors' charging decisions rather than in light of the law's reflection of changes in the sanctioned boundaries of conduct toward women. For society at large, the law may indeed have contributed to enlightened attitudes about rape. But the symbolic impact of the law within the system, if any, seems to be overwhelmed by the importance of technical procedural changes.

To examine this observation in more detail, we regrouped the responses to this question according to whether they pertained primarily to evidence requirements revised under the criminal sexual conduct statute. These include the exclusion of sexual his-

Table 4–10   "Evidentiary" Change by Occupational Role

| Actor Group | Percentage Citing Evidentiary Change |
|---|---|
| Judges (N = 32) | 75.0 |
| Prosecutors (N = 38) | 92.1 |
| Defense Attorneys (N = 29) | 82.8 |
| Police (N = 37) | 67.6 |
| Crisis Center Staff (N = 24) | 75.0 |
| Total (N = 160) | 78.8 |

tory evidence, the removal of the need to prove "resistance to the utmost," or the elimination of need for corroborating witnesses.

Table 4–10 shows that over three-fourths of all respondents thought that changes in evidence requirements were among the law's most significant features; the attention given to the sexual history exclusion is predominant. Role demands of particular actor groups seem to account for the slight differences that emerge. Predictably, as a group, prosecutors (92 percent) named some aspect of evidentiary reform more often than did others. Police are less inclined than others to feel that the exclusion of sexual history evidence is important, but they were more impressed than others with the change in corroboration requirements. None of the defense attorneys cited corroboration requirements as among the law's most important features.

Respondents' perceptions of the significant aspects of the law have implications for other states that have passed legislation or are considering legislation similar to Michigan's. While the limitation on sexual history evidence is clearly critical, the degree structure and changes in codification and terminology contribute importantly, facilitating a different approach to sexual assault cases. With rare exceptions, the assessments were voiced regardless of respondents' vantage point in the system; there seems to be wide agreement among and between groups as to the significance of these procedural changes.

Perhaps because Michigan's statute is a "sweeping revision," respondents believe that it has brought changes both in the criminal justice system and in social norms regarding women and rape. Because the law radically restructures case processing, it has focused attention on itself—and on the rape issue—which seems to have encouraged its adoption. The responses to our initial interview question about the significant aspects of the law attest to the fact that respondents are not only aware of the law but supportive of the specific procedural changes specified in its provisions.

## Summary

Overall our data lead to the conclusion that implementation of the law is expressed primarily in specific procedural changes, not in institutional reform. Judges believe that juries are more enlightened now, but in general we observed changes in case processing without concomitant "symbolic" changes such as a redefinition of the crime. These two threads—specific procedural changes and overall attitudinal stability—run throughout our examination of the changes that the law has produced. For example, respondents believe that the law had fulfilled its intention of exerting control over decision making by restricting sexual history evidence. While this provision of the law is exceptionally influential, sexual history evidence is sometimes still admitted improperly or introduced through innuendo. The option to hold *in-camera* hearings to establish the relevance of such information, and perhaps to rule it out when not appropriate, is largely not exercised. Prosecutors can now win cases more easily, and the importance of certain elements of the crime has diminished. But neither prosecutors nor defense attorneys have substantially altered their courtroom tactics, and defense attorneys report that for the most part they still actively seek information about a complainant's sex past. And the victim's character and credibility remain the central focus of the CSC case.

In general, the findings from interviews with officials suggest that the law has very little impact on the system's approach to sexual assault cases, despite statistical improvements in conviction rates. Its most salutary effects appear to be reserved for those outside the system—the sexual assault victims themselves. And it also has a profound effect on another group outside the system—defendants who are now more often convicted and imprisoned.

## Endnotes

1. Only 7 respondents of the 165 who answered this question failed to mention at least one of the reasons that would suggest an increase in sexual assault reports rather than an increase in the crime's incidence. Our findings contrast with those of a 1977 study by the National Institute for Law Enforcement and Criminal Justice. In their survey of prosecutors, primarily in states without revised rape laws, 76 percent named a general increase in violence as the reason for the jump in reporting rates. In Michigan, only a third of prosecutors mentioned an increase in violence as contributing to reports, and among all respondents it was ranked fifth.

2. Lest respondents be accused of self-congratulation, it is important to keep in mind that, even with the publicity that accompanied the law reform, the general population is probably unaware of the change. Respondents are in a position to know whether average victims are familar with the new statute, and apparently they are not.

3. Virginia B. Nordby, "Legal Effects of Proposed Rape Reform Bills." Mimeograph (April 1974).

4. On the other hand, two-thirds of rape crisis center staff thought prosecutors had changed their tactics. The observations of the prosecutors and judges are probably more accurate than those of the crisis center staff. Most rape crisis centers are relatively young organizations, so staff members interviewed had limited pre-CSC law experience with which to compare current prosecutor behavior. Their response may primarily reflect optimism about the potential of law reform activities.

5. Harry Kalven and Hans Zeisel, *The American Jury* (Chicago: University of Chicago Press, 1966); Eugene Borgida, "Evidentiary Reform of Rape Laws: A Psycholegal Approach," in P.D. Lipsett and B.D. Sales (eds.), *New Directions in Psycholegal Research* (New York: Van Nostrand Reinhold, 1978).

*Chapter 5*

# THE DYNAMICS OF CHANGE: LAW REFORM FOR WHOM?

So far we have discussed respondents' perception of change in terms of the procedural alterations the Michigan law introduced into the criminal justice system. But it was concern with the status and treatment of victims in the criminal justice system that served as a major impetus for the reform. In the crime of rape more blatantly than in others, efforts to protect defendants' rights often seriously infringe on those of victims. The authors of the statute were compelled by more than interest in procedural changes, which were only the means by which to achieve a larger goal. They reasoned that implementation of the provisions of the statute would substantially reduce the harassment and degradation of victims who report sexual assaults and seek legal redress through the courts.

Quantitative analysis of official crime statistics shed little light on the issue of victim experience. Implementation without improvements in victims' experience would have been an empty accomplishment. We therefore sought the views of respondents regarding this critically important measure of the law's effectiveness. We asked them specifically to identify whether or not they observed improvements in victims' experience and increases in cases not covered under previous statutes—that is, male rape and legally separated spouses. Finally, we asked them about the impact of the law on defendants' rights: Does the law in any way violate defendants' rights?

From the perspective of respondents, the law has reduced victims' trauma in the criminal justice system principally—but not exclusively—because it prohibits testimony about victims' sex past. Furthermore, respondents agree that the law has encouraged victims to report cases not covered under previous statutes. When the system pursues these cases, respondents perceive that victims have a better chance of achieving convictions than they did previously. But in terms of successful prosecution, the category in which respondents describe the most change are those cases in which evidence of the complainant's sexual history would have prejudiced the outcome. For the most part, respondents agree with the Michigan courts that the improvements for victims have not jeopardized defendants' rights.

## Perceived Changes in Victim Experience Attributable to the Law

Victims themselves, not criminal justice officials, could provide the most accurate picture of changes in their treatment since the law took effect. But most victims fortunately lack an historical view, and most, we felt, would not wish to recount the details of their experience. Members of the criminal justice system and crisis centers have observed the treatment of victims both before and after the law reform, and they serve as well-placed informants for judging whether victim experience with the system has changed. Regardless of their vantage point within the system, the overwhelming majority (82 percent) of these respondents agreed that the victim's experience in the criminal justice system is less traumatic under the new law. Only 15 percent (Table 5-1) believe that the victim's experience has not changed, and a few respondents thought that it had actually deteriorated.

While the majority of all respondent groups were positive, crisis center staff are unanimous in their assertion that the victim's experience has improved and judges are most equivocal. Proximity to the victim and the crime may explain differences among these groups' appraisals. With the possible exception of police officers, crisis center staff are most familiar with the details of the victim's experience. These counselors often spend time with victims before they receive medical attention; they accompany them to the

Table 5–1  Relationship of Occupational Role to View of the Victim's Experience as More or Less Traumatic (N = 157)

| Occupational Role | Percentage of Respondents | | |
|---|---|---|---|
| | More Traumatic | Unchanged | Less Traumatic |
| Judge (N = 31) | 3.1 | 28.1 | 68.8 |
| Prosecutor (N = 39) | 5.0 | 17.5 | 77.5 |
| Defense Attorney (N = 29) | 6.7 | 6.7 | 86.7 |
| Police (N = 36) | 0 | 13.9 | 86.1 |
| Crisis Center (N = 22) | 0 | 0 | 100.0 |
| Total | 3.2 | 14.6 | 82.2 |

emergency room and guide them through the labyrinth of the criminal justice system. They encouraged law reform originally because the old law precluded the possibility that victims could receive fair treatment in the courts. Perhaps because they actively pursued the law's passage, they have few reservations about the law; their view of its effect on victim experience reflects this enthusiasm.

But several respondents suggested that these counselors, most of whom lack experience with the old law, have an exaggerated view of the treatment of victims in the past. They contend that improvements are less dramatic than crisis centers believe because, as one prosecutor put it, "People's worst fears (about the system) weren't true."[1]

The majority of respondents in all counties believed the victim's experience had improved. Table 5–2 would seem to indicate that,

Table 5–2  Relationship of County to View of the Victim's Experience as More or Less Traumatic (N = 157)

| County | Percentage of Respondents | | |
|---|---|---|---|
| | More Traumatic | Unchanged | Less Traumatic |
| A (N = 10) | 0 | 18.2 | 81.8 |
| B (N = 16) | 9.1 | 9.1 | 81.8 |
| C (N = 14) | 0 | 13.3 | 86.7 |
| D (N = 15) | 0 | 11.8 | 88.2 |
| E (N = 21) | 4.5 | 18.2 | 77.3 |
| F (N = 85) | 3.7 | 14.8 | 81.5 |
| Total | 3.2 | 14.6 | 82.2 |

Table 5–3   **Relationship of Occupational Role to Factors Considered the Most Important Contribution to Improved Victim Experience (N = 117)**

| Occupational Role | Restriction on Past Sexual History | No Need to Prove Nonconsent | No Need to Prove Resistance | Crisis Center Support | Changed Social Attitudes | Treatment by Police | Female Police Officers | Other |
|---|---|---|---|---|---|---|---|---|
| | *Percentage of Respondents* | | | | | | | |
| Judge (N = 20) | 65.0 | 5.0 | 5.0 | 5.0 | 5.0 | 5.0 | 0 | 10.0 |
| Prosecutor (N = 31) | 45.2 | 0 | 6.5 | 16.1 | 22.6 | 6.5 | 0 | 3.2 |
| Defense Attorney (N = 23) | 39.1 | 4.3 | 4.3 | 17.4 | 21.7 | 8.7 | 0 | 4.3 |
| Police (N = 21) | 47.6 | 0 | 14.3 | 4.8 | 14.3 | 0 | 9.5 | 9.5 |
| Crisis Center (N = 22) | 31.8 | 4.5 | 9.5 | 18.6 | 27.3 | 4.5 | 4.5 | 0 |
| Total | 45.3 | 2.6 | 7.7 | 12.8 | 18.8 | 5.1 | 2.6 | 5.1 |

regardless of jurisdictional differences, the law's effect is pervasive, reducing the difficulties victims previously encountered while pursuing a case.

## Legal and Institutional Factors Influencing Victim Experience

Among those who reported that the victim's experience has improved, nearly half attribute the improvement to one characteristic of the law: prohibition of evidence related to past sexual conduct. Nineteen percent of the respondents believed a change in attitudes toward women and sexual assault was most important in explaining the improvement, and 13 percent said crisis center support was crucial. But as Tables 5–3 and 5–4 show, across all actors and all counties restriction on sexual history evidence emerges as the key to perceived improvement.

Prosecutors, defense attorneys, and crisis center staff frequently mentioned that crisis center support and changed social attitudes had lessened victim trauma. Police, on the other hand, thought crisis center support was less important than change in resistance requirements. Police officers know only too well that in a great many situations resistance by the victim is ill-advised. Without the need for evidence of resistance, police officers clearly have more flexibility to seek warrants for arrest. It is also possible that the relative indifference of the police to the influence of crisis centers may reflect the historically adversarial relationship of these groups.

In Table 5–4 factors reported as contributing to improved victim experience are displayed by county. Beyond the fact that respondents in all counties consider the restriction of evidence of sexual history to be crucial, differences emerge across counties. Changes in social attitudes are viewed as important in all but one county, the least populous in the sample. Crisis center support appears to be valued in larger, more urban counties. Perhaps this is because the demands of case processing are such that criminal justice system officials are overwhelmed and turn to crisis centers to help the victim. In the rural county (County A), which lacks a crisis center, improvements are attributed to features of the statute (elimination of the requirements to prove nonconsent and resistance) and to the work of female police officers.

**Table 5–4   Relationship of County to Factors Considered the Most Important Contribution to Improved Victim Experience (N = 117)**

| | Percentage of Respondents | | | | | | | |
| County | Restriction on Past Sexual History | No Need to Prove Nonconsent | No Need to Prove Resistance | Crisis Center Support | Changed Social Attitudes | Treatment by Police | Female Police Officers | Other |
|---|---|---|---|---|---|---|---|---|
| A (N = 9) | 55.6 | 11.1 | 11.1 | 0 | 0 | 0 | 11.1 | 11.1 |
| B (N = 11) | 54.5 | 0 | 9.1 | 0 | 27.3 | 0 | 9.1 | 0 |
| C (N = 10) | 30.0 | 10.0 | 0 | 30.0 | 30.0 | 0 | 0 | 0 |
| D (N = 12) | 50.1 | 0 | 8.3 | 8.3 | 25.0 | 8.3 | 0 | 0 |
| E (N = 17) | 35.3 | 5.9 | 5.9 | 17.6 | 23.5 | 0 | 0 | 11.8 |
| F (N = 58) | 46.6 | 0 | 8.6 | 13.8 | 15.5 | 8.6 | 1.1 | 5.2 |
| Total | 48.3 | 2.6 | 7.7 | 12.8 | 18.8 | 5.1 | 2.6 | 5.2 |

Those who perceived that the victim's experience had improved because of extralegal factors cited police sensitivity, public consciousness, and crisis center support as being most influential. Many credited women police officers with a more sympathetic approach. Others said that changes in the law and the criminal justice system were not substantive, but that social change made victims less likely to be stigmatized. A prosecutor stated, "I don't think the damn system's any more sensitive. But victims are more willing to speak about sexual matters." A defense attorney who perceived little change in the system said, "Women have generally come to realize that it is not a disgrace to be the victim of a sexual deviate—they realize that it simply was not their fault."

The respondents most eager to explain their position were those who thought that the victim's experience in the criminal justice system had not changed. For several, the nature of the criminal justice system militates against improvements. A defense attorney said, "Society still treats women as objects—and that is reflected in the courts." Another added, "The court system is such that the victim is the second most screwed in any case—after the defendant."

In a similar vein, a prosecutor explained:

*The law helps the prosecution, but I don't think it helps the victim at all. Nothing can prevent that trauma. If you treat a sex crime as a crime, then the victim has to go through what everyone does in the criminal justice system. She must go into a courtroom, face cross-examination and the trauma associated with an act of violence, an especially degrading one. B and E (breaking and entering) isn't the same as rape when you have to describe what happened. There's nothing the criminal sexual conduct statute can do to alleviate that. You can never change it.*

Some respondents believe that a sexual assault is so traumatic that changes in the law or the legal system can only be cosmetic. According to a police officer, "It's the worst experience you'll ever have in your life, no matter what the laws are." And a defense attorney said, "It was traumatic under the old law and it still is. It's like choosing between Armageddon and the Holocaust."

## Perceived Effects of the Law's Expanded Coverage

The reformers viewed the law as a means to extend legal protection to groups not covered under the old law. Specifically, they sought to protect males, incest victims, and victims who were raped by spouses from whom they were legally separated. The expanded definition of the crime, articulated both in the evidentiary provisions and in the kinds of offenses included, now covers victims involved in "marginal" cases (lacking prompt report, corroborating evidence or both) and victims raped by anyone with whom they had a prior relationship, whether casual or sexually intimate.[2]

Two-thirds of the respondents (67 percent) felt that there had been a change in the types of cases getting into the criminal justice system since the passage of the law. Twenty-three percent simply described an overall increase in sexual assault cases, an increase which could be independent of the law. But when specific kinds of cases were mentioned, the effects of the law itself become clear. Table 5–5 shows the frequency with which various types of cases are mentioned by respondents as having increased under the CSC statute.

Over one-fourth of the respondents (28.3 percent) describe an increase in incest cases, and one in five (20.7) cite an increase in

Table 5–5  Types of Cases That Have Increased Since the Law Reform (N = 48)

| Type of Cases | Percentage of Respondents Mentioning Type of Case |
|---|---|
| Involving members of the same family (incest) | 28.3 |
| Involving separated spouses | 20.7 |
| In which victim is under 13 years | 20.7 |
| Involving victim and defendant of same sex | 18.8 |
| Involving "marginal" facts or evidence | 13.2 |
| In which victim and defendant were previously acquainted | 7.5 |
| In which victim and defendant had a previous sexual relationship | 1.9 |
| In which victim was willing to pursue complaint | 1.9 |
| General increase in cases | 22.6 |

NOTE: Because respondents were allowed up to two responses to this question, total responses exceed 100 percent.

"statutory rapes." The law specifies two situations in which the age of the victim can serve as an aggravating factor. The first is any circumstance in which the victim is under the age of thirteen years. The second is when the defendant either lives with, is related to, or is in a position of authority over a victim between the ages of thirteen and sixteen years. The intent of the legislature to clarify the criminal law and provide reasonable guidelines for the courts is clearly illustrated by this aspect of the law. These changes were motivated in part by a desire to protect young people (particularly young males) from false charges by third parties such as parents.

At the time the law was passed, there was some concern that reduction of the age of consent from sixteen to thirteen would provide too little protection for young women. The increase in these types of cases, even under the revised requirements, suggests that those fears were unfounded. The statute's clarity in this area has obviously contributed to the increased frequency with which sexual assaults of children, whether by a relative or stranger, are receiving attention from the criminal justice system. The sharp increase in incest cases also raises questions about the actual incidence of the crime and the role of law in bringing it into the public domain. Our data clearly illustrate the value a legal revision can bring to the reporting and prosecution of incest cases but do not allow us to speculate with certainty about their fate in the absence of a statutory reform. It is possible that incest is on the increase; several police officers and crisis center workers said that their incest caseloads alone left them little time to pursue other investigations. It is equally possible that these cases may have come to authorities' attention in the past, only to be turned away because the previous law was too vague to cover the circumstances and to enable prosecution to occur.

The Michigan law protects spouses living apart when one has filed for separate maintenance or divorce, and a sizable proportion of respondents (21 percent) mentioned that they now handle these cases. Most victims who now bring charges would have been unable to do so under previous statutes. Even the limited protection extended to separated spouses in the CSC law is strongly justified by the frequency with which this group is now seen in the criminal justice system.

A substantial number of respondents (18.8 percent) reported

that the criminal justice system now handles more cases involving male victims. Sexual assaults of males were previously prosecuted under a vague sodomy law. Pursuant to equal protection and anticipating passage of the Equal Rights Amendment, male victims of any sexual assault and of any age are now protected.

Sexual assaults involving children, legally separated spouses, and male victims were previously prosecuted under a variety of laws. But former statutes simply did not create an opportunity to systematically prosecute these assaults following comprehensive, clear, and uniform rules of evidence. The new law recognizes all of these as sexual assaults containing parallel elements. Its implementation—and its effectiveness—in this regard are supported by respondents' observations of increases in these specific types of cases. The data also give evidence that the handling of sexual assault cases has been normalized to some extent. No matter who is victimized, the statute provides that consistent standards of law are applied to cases whose circumstances fall along a continuum of sexual violence.

But respondents also mentioned increases in cases that might technically have been prosecuted under the previous forcible rape statutes. Many of these cases are still considered "marginal" for a variety of reasons that made—and still make—successful prosecution less certain: a lack of prompt complaint, for instance, or a weak link in the chain of evidence. In the past, these cases might not have been pursued. Thirteen percent of our respondents have noted an increase in such "marginal" cases under the new law. Similarly, respondents report that cases in which victims and defendants have had some prior relationship, whether casual or intimate, are now reaching the criminal justice system in greater numbers. These cases also could have been prosecuted under previous statutes but in fact rarely were; the increase results from the most widely acclaimed aspect of the statute, the evidentiary provision and the resulting shift away from preoccupation with the victim's character.

The law further does not require the prosecution to show that the victim resisted, nor does it require the corroboration of victim's testimony. The prosecution must prove that force was used, but it does not have to prove nonconsent. The defendant may still raise the consent issue, but the use of the victim's sexual history to prove consent is severely limited. Factors such as lack of prompt report or previous relationship between the victim and defendant are therefore not as likely to diminish the prosecution's chances of winning a case.

It is probable that the evidentiary provisions in the new law are responsible for the observation by a few respondents that more victims are willing to prosecute. They report that the limitation on the use of sexual history as evidence, in particular, has made victims less reluctant to seek convictions. For example, one prosecutor said,

> *I sense that there is some increase (in reports) because women feel more confident that the court isn't an arena. For instance, a married woman sees herself as respectable, but she may have a skeleton in the closet. Now, she'll bring charges because judges, police and eventually juries will be more empathetic [sic] with her situation.*

The possibility of maintaining some privacy while pursuing a sexual assault case lends some reasonableness to what is not an easy experience under any circumstances. Some prosecutors and police capitalize on this insight. Three-quarters of the respondents reported that they "sometimes" or "frequently" advise victims about evidentiary provisions in the new law in order to encourage them to prosecute.

When the reformed legislation passed in Michigan, there was concern that if the law pulled more types of cases, particularly "marginal" ones, into the system, fewer convictions overall would be achieved. As discussed previously, neither crime statistics nor interview data support that view. We asked what kinds of cases resulted in guilty verdicts now when they would have resulted in acquittal before, and prosecutors themselves mentioned cases with marginal sets of facts. Other cases cited typically related to specific characteristics of the statute or to victim characteristics. The percentage of respondents describing these cases is presented in Table 5–6.

The most frequently mentioned category of cases (58 percent of respondents) which can now be prosecuted successfully includes those in which the victim's sexual history could have been prejudicial to the outcome. For instance, 4 percent of the respondents described cases in which the defendant was found guilty of sexually assaulting a prostitute. Others can be successfully pursued now because the specific language of the law makes

Table 5–6    Types of Cases Won After Law Reform That Could Not Have
             Been Won Prior to Law Reform (N = 44)

| Type of Case | Percentage of Respondents |
|---|---|
| Cases with prejudicial sexual history information | 57.8 |
| Cases specifically defined by new law that were not included in old law | 15.6 |
| Cases that could not have met resistance requirement of previous laws | 13.3 |
| Cases involving poor judgment on part of victim | 13.3 |
| Cases involving lack of prompt report | 8.9 |
| Cases involving male victims | 6.7 |
| Cases in which victim is a prostitute | 4.4 |
| Cases involving legally separated spouses | 2.2 |

NOTE: Because multiple responses to this question were allowed, total responses exceed 100 percent.

explicit the criminality of certain acts not formerly included in the statutes. Respondents are also achieving convictions for cases in which it would have been difficult to prove resistance and non-consent—demands no longer made of the prosecution (Table 5–6).

The most noteworthy cases described, however, are those "marginal" cases that can be won now because personal characteristics of the victim no longer play such a central role. Thirteen percent of respondents described cases in which the victim used poor judgment—for example, accepted a ride from a stranger—and 9 percent had achieved convictions in cases in which the crime was not promptly reported. These circumstances, which even now may hinder prosecution, previously spelled certain acquittal in sexual assault cases.

## Perceived Impact on Defendant's Rights

Of course, the CSC statute profoundly affects another group of people: those accused of the crime. Critics of rape law reforms, as well as their authors, have been concerned that these laws preserve the constitutional rights of defendants. In Michigan, various members of the criminal justice system, particularly defense attorneys, argued against passage of the law on constitutional grounds.

When we asked judges, prosecutors, and defense attorneys whether they believed that the new law violated defendants' constitutional rights, only 14 percent (most of these defense attorneys) felt that it "definitely" violated them. Table 5–7 shows that an overwhelming majority of prosecutors (95 percent) and judges (84 percent) considered the law within constitutional limits. One prosecutor succinctly put the issue into perspective when he said,

> *The constitutional requirement at stake is confrontation. There is no constitutional right to confront about everything lousy or indiscreet or fun that the witness ever did.*

On the other hand, nearly three-fourths of the defense attorneys (73 percent) disagreed with the majority view. Only one of seventy-one prosecutors and judges believed that the law "definitely violated" defendants' rights, while 43 percent of the thirty defense attorneys felt that the law "definitely violated" these rights.

Those who believed the law violated defendants' rights most commonly cited the restriction of evidence of victims' sexual history as an abridgment of defendants' Sixth Amendment right to confront witnesses against them. Others claimed that the law is unconstitutionally vague and mentioned prosecutors' use of the law to bring multiple charges against a defendant when there was only one penetration or sexual contact. The latter practice, they

Table 5–7   **Respondents' Beliefs about the Constitutionality of Michigan's CSC Law**

| Percent who Believe the Law . . . | Judges (N = 32) | Prosecutors (N = 39) | Defense Attorneys (N = 30) | Total (N =101) |
|---|---|---|---|---|
| Definitely violates defendants' rights | 3.1% (1) | 0.0% (0) | 43.3% (13) | 13.9% (14) |
| Probably violates defendants' rights | 12.5 (4) | 5.1 (2) | 30.0 (9) | 14.9 (15) |
| Probably does not violate defendants' rights | 37.5 (12) | 41.0 (16) | 16.7 (5) | 32.7 (33) |
| Definitely does not violate defendants' rights | 46.9 (15) | 53.9 (21) | 10.0 (3) | 38.5 (39) |
| Total | 100.0% (32) | 100.0% (39) | 100.0% (30) | 100.0% (101) |

felt, was a violation of the constitutional protection against double jeopardy.[3]

As generally happens with any legal revision, the constitutionality of Michigan's law has been challenged in the courts numerous times since it took effect in 1975. To date, no important provision of the law itself has been deemed unconstitutional. The practice of charging multiple counts of CSC where there is a single penetration or sexual contact, however, has been held to be improper on other than constitutional grounds.

Some defendants have argued that various features of the new law deny them due process in that certain provisions are unconstitutionally vague (*People v. Clark*, 85 Mich. App. 96 [1978]) or overly broad (*People v. Dalton*, 83 Mich. App. 725 [1978]). In each of these cases the law has been unanimously upheld. At least one defendant has also tried to convince the Michigan Appellate Court that the CSC law unconstitutionally denied equal protection to males (*People v. McDonald*, 86 Mich. App. 5 [1978]). The court found this defendant's contention to be unwarranted in a unanimous decision.

The most controversial provision of Michigan's CSC law, the sexual history exclusion, is probably also its most important. As noted above, among those who believed that the law violates defendants' rights, over 80 percent believe this provision to be unconstitutional. Thus far, the Michigan courts of appeals have upheld the prohibition in every challenge, but the Michigan Supreme Court has yet to consider this issue.

Briefly, the arguments that prohibit evidence of a victim's sexual history center around two issues: (1) whether or not such evidence might be probative of credibility, and (2) whether or not it might be probative of consent. The courts have had less difficulty disposing of the credibility issue than the consent issue. A few appellate judges seem to feel that cases could arise in which evidence of a victim's sexual history might be more than remotely relevant to the issue of consent and that the law is therefore too rigid in precluding all sexual history evidence (see, for example, Judge Kaufman in *People v. Thompson*, 76 Mich. App. 705 [1977]). Judge Cavanaugh suggests that *in-camera* hearings be used by trial judges to determine if certain sexual history evidence (beyond that currently admissible under 520j[2] of the CSC law) is relevant and should be admitted. Most Michigan appellate judges, on the other hand, seem to believe that instances where this evidence might be relevant to either credibility or consent are inconceivable, or that its slight relevance would be outweighed by society's interests in protecting victims from usually pointless and sometimes cruel questioning and in encouraging victims to prosecute (see, for example, *People v. Thompson*, 76 Mich. App. 705, 712).

There has been one case in which a less important aspect of this part of the law has been ruled unconstitutional by a Michigan court. In a two-to-one decision, a court of appeals ruled in 1980 that it was an unconstitutional denial of defendant's Sixth Amendment right to confrontation to require the defense attorney to give ten days' notice of the intent to question a complainant about her past sexual relations with the accused (*People v. Williams*, 95 Mich. App. 1 [1980]). The prosecutor in the case appealed the decision to the Michigan Supreme Court.

The final area of the CSC law that has been challenged on constitutional grounds pertains to the practice of bringing multiple charges, described above. In this instance the Michigan Supreme Court has ruled in favor of the defendant, but it has done so based on legal rather than constitutional grounds. In *People v. Johnson* (SC 60015, June 18, 1979), the court held that even though a single sexual penetration may be accompanied by more than one of the aggravating circumstances enumerated in the CSC law, it may give rise to only one criminal charge for purposes of trial, conviction, or sentencing. The court went on to state, however, that this does not preclude a prosecutor from listing in all information each of the aggravating circumstances, nor from arguing the separate circumstantial bases upon which a jury can return a verdict on a single count. The court reached its decision based upon its interpretation of the CSC law and the intent of the legislature in passing it. While ruling against a practice of some prosecutors, this decision does not undermine the letter or intent of the CSC law.

Undoubtedly, there will be further challenges to rape law reforms, whether proposed or already enacted. But most respondents agree with the courts that the CSC statute extends greater protection to a greater number of victims without abridging the constitutional rights of the defendant.

## Was the Law Necessary?

A nagging concern throughout the evaluation of the law reform derived from realization that the changes detected could have happened in the absence of the legal reform. We took this concern to our criminal justice system respondents. An overwhelming majority (75 percent) felt that Michigan's criminal sexual conduct statute was a necessary revision. Again they emphasized that, by prohibiting sexual history evidence, the law improves the victim's experience in the criminal justice system. Some did not refer to a specific provision but believed that the law had generally helped the victim. For instance, from one judge's perspective,

> *The old law was very outdated, especially statutory rape. The courtroom and sentencing procedures had reached a point where the victim needed a break. And she got a break under the new law.*

As Table 5–8 shows in more detail, respondents were impressed with other features of Michigan's statute, such as its clarity and degree structure, its changes in resistance and consent standards, and the terminology it employs. A substantial proportion of respondents said that a new law was needed primarily to influence or to reflect emerging social awareness about sexual assault, and

Table 5–8    Respondents' Views of Why the Criminal Sexual Conduct Law
Was Necessary (N = 127)

| Respondents' Views | Percentage of Respondents Mentioning View |
|---|---|
| Restricts use of sexual history evidence | 30.7 |
| Reflects or changes society's view of rape | 18.1 |
| Improves victim experience | 17.3 |
| Statute is logical and comprehensive | 17.3 |
| Degree structure outlines charges and sentences | 15.7 |
| Changes resistance and consent standards | 15.0 |
| Defines terminology and codifies | 14.2 |
| Lowers age of consent | 7.1 |
| Alters criminal justice processing procedures | 5.5 |
| Makes conviction easier | 4.7 |
| Is gender neutral | 2.4 |
| Protects separated spouses | 0.8 |

NOTE: Because respondents were allowed up to two responses to this question, total responses exceed 100 percent.

several specifically mentioned that the law reform effort was necessary because it generated publicity about the crime.

In assessing the need for Michigan's law, nearly half the respondents gave attention to features of the law related primarily to technical and procedural issues. Among these were the law's clear and comprehensive articulation of criminally assaultive behaviors, and its degree structure, designed to facilitate police investigation, prosecutors' charging and plea-bargaining decisions, and judges' sentencing options. And several respondents noted that the law made it easier to achieve convictions.

Their remarks in this regard seem to address the importance and value of taking into account the entrenched features of the system when seeking to maximize a proposed law's potential. Overall the respondents seem to believe that the law was a prerequisite to positive developments in rape case processing since 1975. Where it did not specifically alter procedures, it fostered an awareness of the issue that prodded changes along. Describing the reasons a new law was needed, a prosecutor simply said, "The common law of rape was atrocious. It prosecuted or seemed to put the victim on trial."

## Summary

While still a difficult experience, the victim's interaction with the criminal justice system has improved as a result of the law reform. The reports of our respondents indicate further that victims are able to pursue cases not covered under previous statutes: incest cases, male rape, and those involving legally separated spouses. The chances of achieving convictions for these cases are good, but they have improved most dramatically for cases that were covered under the old law but damaged by admissibility of evidence of complainants' sexual history. Moreover, respondents determined that these advances had not come at the expense of defendants' rights. The law has, at this point, met all constitutional challenges.

The interview data indicate the importance of the statute for victims of sexual assault crimes; the crime data point to the value of the law in improving the effectiveness of case processing. And, while acknowledging that these and related changes could have been accomplished through other means respondents specified aspects of the law that made it not only important but necessary for these achievements.


## Endnotes

1. A recent study indicates that, in fact, the victim's experience in the court-room varies according to the defense strategy used. It is most difficult when the defense is consent. However, when the defense is, for example, identification (that is, that someone else committed the crime), victim characteristics play a much smaller role. See Barbara Reskin, Marie Matthews, Stephanie Sanford, Christy Visker, and Gary LaFree, "Studying Jury Verdicts in Sexual Assault Cases: Some Preliminary Findings." Paper presented at the 1980 Meetings of the American Society of Criminology (San Francisco, 1980).
2. The legislation as proposed by the Michigan Women's Task Force on Rape also included the protection of married women, but this was compromised out in the legislature.
3. Some prosecutors in Michigan have charged defendants with more than one offense, even when only one penetration or sexual contact occurred, if the conduct could be included under more than one of the different specifications within any of the four degrees of criminal sexual conduct. For example, if a defendant penetrated a victim once, but was armed, used force, and caused injury to the victim, a prosecutor might charge the defendant with two counts of CSC in the first degree—one under Sec. 520b(1)(e) and a second under Sec. 520b(1)(f) of the statute (see The Law, Appendix B).

*Chapter 6*

# IMPEDIMENTS TO IMPLEMENTATION

Law primarily governs the conduct of the most visible aspect of a case, its culmination in trial. But it leaves untouched many steps in case processing that are crucial to determining whether a case ever reaches the courtroom. Based on our interview data, we believe that there are junctures in the investigation at which the rape victim confronts a unique skepticism in the form of institutionalized policies and practices the law did not address. These reflect both enduring myths about the crime and unchallenged bureaucratic routines.

We asked respondents to discuss decision-making steps that typically characterize the process by which a sexual assault report leads to an investigation, issuance of an arrest warrant, and eventually a case that comes before a judge and/or jury. These early stages in case processing are rarely monitored by outsiders, and all involve discretionary decisions by police and prosecutors.

We asked about these phases of case processing despite some concern that respondents might not give veridical reports of what transpires. In the absence of objective data sources, we describe the responses here as the best available evidence concerning whether professionals use a different approach to CSC cases when discretion, not the law, is the guide.

## Factors Influencing the Decision to Pursue a Case

As discussed in Chapter 3, there was little change in the rate of unfoundings of reported rapes in Michigan between 1972 and 1978. Demonstrating remarkably reliable judgment with respect to the statistics, most police said that less than 10 percent of reported rapes are unfounded, and the majority (72 percent) perceived quite accurately that the CSC law had not changed the rate of unfoundings.[1]

To determine whether CSC reports are more prone to rejection by police, we asked them to compare unfounding rates in sexual assaults with those in equally serious crimes. Apparently, police officers believe sexual assault reports to be at least as reliable as those of other serious crimes.[2]

In order to ascertain whether unique criteria were used to determine the validity of CSC complaints, we asked police officers to rank a set of items considered in making such a decision, and then to rank the same items as they might apply to the report of an equally serious crime. As shown in Table 6–1, the items had the same relative importance, with a few notable exceptions. "Suspect identification" was less often a problem in sexual assault cases; it is estimated that victims and defendants know one another in one-third to one-half of the cases.[3] And the "lack of a corroborating witness" is less often a reason to reject a rape com-

Table 6–1    Relative Importance of Various Factors in Determining a Complaint to Be Unfounded in Criminal Sexual Conduct (CSC) and Equally Serious Crimes (ESC) (N = 37 Police)

| Factor | CSC (rank order) | ESC (rank order) |
|---|---|---|
| Victim fails a polygraph | 1 | 1 |
| Suspect passes a polygraph | 2 | 2 |
| Victim withdraws complaint | 3 | 4 |
| Inconsistencies in complainant's story | 4 | 3 |
| Suspect has a good alibi | 5 | 5 |
| Poor personal credibility of complainant | 6 | 8 |
| Lack of physical evidence | 7 | 7 |
| Problems with suspect identification | 8 | 6 |
| Lack of prompt complaint | 9 | 10 |
| No documented physical injury | 10 | 11 |
| Lack of corroborating witness | 11 | 9 |

plaint because there is so rarely a witness that the police do not expect one.[4]

Because witnesses are unusual, the police and subsequently prosecutors and a judge or jury rely heavily on the perceived veracity of the victim's testimony. It is, therefore, not difficult to appreciate why "poor personal credibility" of the complainant is more frequently cited as a basis for unfoundings in sexual assault crimes. The "one-on-one" nature of sexual assault crimes, resulting from few witnesses to these crimes, appears to enlarge the importance of the complainant's self-presentation in decisions to investigate a CSC charge. The data suggest that the relatively low unfounding rate for sexual assault crimes may be at the expense of the victim, who must survive rigorous scrutiny and detailed questioning.

## Factors Influencing the Decision to Issue a Warrant

The prosecutor's decision to issue an arrest warrant marks the formal entry of the case into the criminal justice system. Once the police officer has determined the report to be valid, it is taken to the prosecutor who must then decide whether to issue or deny a warrant for the arrest of the suspect. Like the police unfounding decision, the prosecutor's decision *not* to file terminates the involvement of the system with the case. At this time, the police investigator, office policies, and even interest groups may exert influence, but it is essentially the prosecutor who decides whether or not a case is pursued. Because the law leaves room for discretion, and because prosecutors have traditionally been conservative when issuing warrants for sexual assault, we questioned them about the warrant denial decision. Over 70 percent said that they "seldom" denied sexual assault warrant requests, and they generally said that warrant denials were more frequent in other serious crimes. Like police estimates of unfounding rates, these perceptions could indicate that prosecutors approach CSC cases much as they do others and consider sexual assault complaints to be at least as reliable as others.

Prosecutors who said that they pursue more CSC cases than others credited special police sex crimes units with more thorough and reliable investigations. Some issue a greater proportion of CSC warrants because they view it as such a serious offense.

Prosecutors who refused more CSC warrant requests than others provided the conventional explanations: the "one-on-one" nature of the crime; victim credibility problems; and the difficulty of winning these cases. From the prosecutor's point of view, these may indeed be obstacles to the successful conclusion of a CSC case, but technically they are unrelated to prosecution and have little bearing on the legitimacy of the report. A number of prosecutors also said that they turned away a greater proportion of CSC cases because of victims' reluctance to pursue the prosecution to completion. This is indeed a frequent problem. In Detroit, analysis of the Sex Crimes Unit data reveals that virtually half of the CSC cases dismissed are accounted for by the complainant's refusal to prosecute or failure to appear at trial. This is most often the reason prosecutors do not issue a warrant in both CSC and other crimes (see Table 6–2). Also, when ranking factors that contribute to warrant denials in both sexual assaults and other crimes, prosecutors indicated that results of the suspect's polygraph test and the credibility of the complainant remain more important in CSC cases. (See Table 6–3 for a comparison of the importance police and prosecutors place on different items when deciding about the validity of CSC reports.)

Police and prosecutors themselves may discourage prosecution of criminal sexual conduct cases by requiring victims to submit

Table 6–2    Relative Importance of Various Factors to Warrant Denials in Criminal Sexual Conduct (CSC) and Equally Serious Crimes (ESC) (N = 38 Prosecutors)

| Factor | CSC (rank order) | ESC (rank order) |
|---|---|---|
| Victim withdraws complaint | 1 | 1 |
| Victim fails a polygraph | 2 | 2 |
| Suspect passes a polygraph | 3 | 4 |
| Problems with suspect identification | 4 | 3 |
| Poor personal credibility of complainant | 5 | 6 |
| Inconsistencies in complainant's story | 6 | 5 |
| Lack of prompt complaint | 7 | 7 |
| Suspect has a good alibi | 8 | 10 |
| Lack of physical evidence | 9 | 8 |
| No documented physical injury | 10 | 11 |
| Lack of corroborating witness | 11 | 9 |

Table 6–3   Police and Prosecutor Ranking of Factors Important in CSC
Unfoundings and Warrant Denials ( N = 75 )

| Description of Factors | Police Unfoundings (rank order) | Prosecutor Warrant Denials (rank order) |
|---|---|---|
| Victim fails polygraph | 1 | 2 |
| Suspect passes polygraph | 2 | 3 |
| Victim withdraws complaint | 3 | 1 |
| Inconsistencies in complainant's story | 4 | 6 |
| Suspect has good alibi | 5 | 8 |
| Poor personal credibility of complainant | 6 | 5 |
| Lack of physical evidence | 7 | 9 |
| Problems with suspect identification | 8 | 4 |
| Lack of prompt complaint | 9 | 7 |
| No documented physical injury | 10 | 10 |
| Lack of corroborating witness | 11 | 11 |

to polygraph tests. Anti-rape activists charge that detailed interrogations of rape victims are unjustified; criminal justice officials defend it as necessary to obtain adequate evidence. Respondents indicate that in some cases they are testing the victim's tenacity for trials—both literal and figurative—to come. They know that victims will eventually face intensive cross-examination and, if ill-prepared, they may have pursued their cases to no avail. According to one police officer, disputes sometime arise between her office and the prosecutors' office:

> . . . *because prosecutors want to interview the victim before issuing a warrant, and they really badger the victim. They do it to see how (victims) will react on the stand to such treatment. I think it is unnecessary and shouldn't come from the prosecutor.*

The desire to seek a conviction, however strong, may be undermined by the victim's desire to forget the attack and leave its effects behind.

A victim's willingness to pursue prosecution, then, can be eroded by the prerogatives of members of the criminal justice system, by delays in case processing (whether engineered by defense attorneys or simply as the result of an overburdened court system), as well as by the victim's fear of retaliation by the attacker and of social response to rape, which is often far less than supportive of the victim. The CSC statute has little effect on these impediments to prosecution.

## Victim Credibility and the Use of Polygraphs

Historically, prosecutors' caution in pursuing sexual assault cases has been influenced primarily by two factors: First, the perception that it is a crime prone to false accusation; second, a concern with winning cases. Lord Chief Justice Hale, quoted by virtually every legal writer who has discussed rape, summarized this partnership of fears by characterizing rape as a charge "easily to be made and hard to be proved and even harder to be defended" (Hale, 1847).

Convictions were rare under Michigan's former rape statutes. By permitting extensive cross-examination of the complainant and requiring strict resistance standards and corroborating witnesses, the old laws embodied biases that made trials difficult to win. The CSC statute was designed to eliminate these problems, but, as the data have shown, the case may still focus on the victim's character. According to respondents themselves, Michigan's statute has, to some degree, removed the uncertainty of achieving convictions, and an emerging awareness of rape makes it plain that rape is not a charge "easily to be made." The degree structure may guide the prosecutor in deciding to take the case and the evidentiary provision may shift the burden of proof, but personal and professional considerations remain. Winning sexual assault cases is still difficult. When the charge is rape, our data indicate, prosecutors still try to be especially sure that the charge is not easily made.

Some officials may investigate rape charges more thoroughly because they consider these reports prone to fabrication. Nearly a third of criminal justice system officials said that they thought rape reports are more frequently fabricated than others. Judges are particularly skeptical. But, as shown in Table 6–4, most respondents felt that fabrication rates are about the same in CSC cases as in others, and a few even thought that rape reports are more often valid ones.[5] Of particular interest are judges, who thought that rape fabrications are more common. Since judges see a select sample of CSC cases—presumably the strongest ones— why are they the most mistrustful of rape reports? Their isolation may allow them to maintain stereotypes unchecked by reality. These data give no evidence of great suspicion on the part of officials, but to the extent that *any* suspicion exists, any given

Table 6–4   Actor Perceptions of Fabrication in Sexual Assault Compared with Equally Serious Crimes

|  | *Percentage of Respondents* | | |
|---|---|---|---|
| *Actor* | *More Fabrication in CSC* | *Less Fabrication in CSC* | *About the Same* |
| Prosecutors (N = 30) | 33.3 | 23.3 | 43.3 |
| Police (N = 26) | 25.9 | 29.6 | 44.4 |
| Defense Attorney (N = 22) | 22.7 | 9.1 | 68.2 |
| Judges (N = 14) | 42.9 | 14.3 | 42.9 |
| Total (N = 92) | 30.4 | 20.7 | 48.9 |

rape case may face evidence requirements that are excessive relative to other types of crimes.

Perhaps because there is a continuing concern with fabrication, polygraphs remained a crucial investigative tool for police and prosecutors at the time we interviewed them. Polygraph use in CSC cases has been the most visible evidence that the criminal justice system approaches rape as a unique crime, subjecting complainants to standards of veracity not applied to others. As shown in Table 6–5, respondents reported that they used polygraphs considerably more often with sexual assault victims, even though they are important in both CSC and other serious crimes. Prosecutors, police, and crisis center staff gave similar estimates of the frequency of polygraph use. Our findings parallel those in a report of the National Institute for Law Enforcement and Criminal Justice[6] in which 31 percent of a national sample of prosecutors said that they never used polygraphs in sexual assault cases

Table 6–5   Use of Polygraphs as Reported by Police and Prosecutors

| *Frequency with Which Complainant Is Asked to Take a Polygraph* | *Percentage of Police and Prosecutors* | |
|---|---|---|
|  | *CSC (N = 77)* | *ESC (N = 62)* |
| All | 5.2 | 1.6 |
| Most | 16.9 | 6.6 |
| Some | 46.8 | 37.1 |
| Few | 29.9 | 53.2 |
| Never | 21.3 | 1.6 |

while 69 percent reported using them sometimes (63 percent) or routinely (6 percent).

A polygraph is often considered necessary when the assailant used threats rather than force in the attack, or when the victim is alleged to be a prostitute, had known the defendant prior to the rape, or had accompanied him to the scene of the crime. Polygraphs may also be required to test the complainant's commitment. A complainant who agrees to take the test is assumed to be willing to proceed through trial.

When asked to explain the difference between polygraph use in sexual assaults and in equally serious crimes, 70 percent of prosecutors and police named the "one-on-one" (that is, no corroborating witnesses) nature of sexual assault (see Table 6–6). They also cited lack of physical evidence, the victim's previous relationship with the defendant, and problems with the victim's credibility. To elaborate this point, a prosecutor said, "CSC can't be compared with other crimes based on seriousness but on evidence, and it is for this reason that polygraphs are used more frequently in CSC cases."

Police often gave examples of cases which contributed to their belief that sexual assault reports are fabricated more than others which provided justification for their use of polygraphs. One Detroit police officer mentioned several cases in which "a juvenile female with a past record—for truancy, for example—makes a rape report to cover up the real reason for her absence." Another believes that most fabrications "are married women who are running around. She 'cries rape' when her husband finds out." The same respondent, along with numerous others, said he had handled rape reports involving young women who "cry rape" when parents discover them to be sexually active.

Table 6–6  **Reasons Polygraphs Used More Frequently in Sexual Assault Crimes (N = 139)**

| Type of Reason | Percentage of Respondents |
|---|---|
| Lack of corroborating evidence | 70.0 |
| Lack of physical evidence | 25.6 |
| Victim's previous relations with defendant | 17.9 |
| Victim lacks credibility | 15.4 |

NOTE: Because up to two explanations were recorded for each respondent, the total percentage reported exceeds 100.

Still others described cases they do not investigate because retribution or revenge seems the motive for the complaint. One policewoman said, "A girl who had been drinking and had sex with this guy made a report. I think her main concern was that she was pregnant and she wanted her medical bills paid. We get a lot like that." Other respondents cited cases in which women brought rape reports to "get revenge" or as a form of blackmail. Some police had handled cases which in their view were not sexual assaults but "failure to pay"—instances in which a prostitute brings a charge of rape against a customer who does not pay the agreed-upon fee. So-called "date rape" cases were often mentioned as cause for skepticism. One officer said,

*We know from experience that if the warrant request is delayed, "cool-off" time will allow the matter to resolve itself. Many (of these cases) are feuds, where the woman is irritated because she was abused or forced to do something. Yet she won't show up at the (preliminary) exam. They kiss and make up.*

A few respondents said that they encourage complainants to "kiss and make up" when the alleged assailant has had a previous sexual relationship with the woman making the report.

Several police officers related their response to women who may have used "bad judgment." One recalled,

*. . . a couple (of cases) where we found out that the woman was picked up in a van and the man made advances. She made out a complaint when all he'd tried to do was see if she was willing and knocked off when she wasn't.*

The officer discouraged prosecution, "although she left here a little upset. . . ." Another officer said that he considered some cases to be unfounded "when women placed themselves in that position: hitchhiking at 2 a.m. or getting drunk at a bar and going home with him." Similarly, a prosecutor justified the difference in polygraph use:

*. . . in cases where the girl was picked up in a bar, was with an ex-boyfriend, in other words, cases where we have a suspicion it was voluntary. We have an obligation in the office to ferret out cases where the girl is getting revenge or just mad.*

This prosecutor went on to say,

*Generally, I feel that there's an obligation for healthy males to do whatever they can with every girl they come across. If he isn't*

*physical about it, and doesn't go beyond the bounds of propriety, then we won't issue a warrant.*

He did not indicate whether his idea of "the bounds of propriety" are consistent with those defined by the law.

The cases cited above are examples of those in which a polygraph is likely to be required. Sometimes the polygraph is suggested to dissuade the complainant. "When we schedule a polygraph, half the time she comes forth with the truth," according to a police officer from the Detroit area. Another said, "We don't use the polygraph to make the determination (that an assault has occurred). We use it to get defendants *off* the hook, not on it." Another officer requires a polygraph "on all victims to be sure that we have all the details, because it's helpful in getting a warrant and to be sure there are no surprises in court."

The significance of the skepticism police evince in describing these cases should be viewed in light of the conflicting demands they must balance, demands that may contribute to their reluctance to pursue certain cases. Some officers are evaluated on the basis of their arrest records, which might provide an incentive for taking every case brought to their attention. But more important, perhaps, is a good working relationship with the prosecutor. Every warrant request should be the product of careful and even cautious investigation if the officer is to establish legitimacy and credibility with the prosecutor who is interested in winning cases. If the officer brings too many bad or "unwinnable" cases to the prosecutor, the working relationship—and the officer's job—will be difficult. Thus in one county, police officers mentioned that, although they do not like to administer polygraphs in CSC cases, they do so because it is the policy of the chief prosecutor.

We interviewed a number of people (20 percent of respondents) who departed from the conventional belief that rape reports should be approached with caution. Some were more willing to believe rape complainants than people who report other crimes. A Detroit detective said,

*When a sex crime is reported, it is normally very serious. It's one thing to make a false report in order to fleece an insurance company in a breaking and entering, but it's another to be raped. It's embarrassing to have to report it.*

Others were more equivocal: "There are stages of fabrication," one prosecutor said. "An out-and-out lie is rare. It (the incident)

usually starts consensually and ends forcibly." In cases like these, he continued, the victim may be likely to falsify certain aspects of the crime or events which preceded the assault in order to strengthen her case.

Still a third prosecutor felt that fabrications in rape cases were practically nonexistent:

> *The women (who report rapes) have time after time shown them-selves to have good judgment—they are not vindictive or out to get men. I have more problems with men who may disbelieve a whore can be raped. This is a philosophical idea disputed by men, not women.*

Those who share this view seem to be in the minority. Many officials are still likely to view a rape complaint with suspicion in all but the most brutal of cases.[7] This skepticism represents a hurdle the rape victim must overcome if the case is to be taken to court.

As these anecdotes illustrate, a complainant's character remains important. Officials seek causal factors in the complainant's behavior, such as hitchhiking or drinking. A complainant's sexual activity outside of marriage also remains salient for those evaluating a case's validity. The new law clearly has not undone the traditions that characterize rape investigations. Established bureaucratic procedures are buttressed by stereotypes about rape, so discretionary decisions can still work to the victim's disadvantage. But even the fullest implementation of the statute would not result in dramatic changes in the investigative practices we examined, because the law does not address these unspoken rules and essentially invisible decisions.

## Individual versus Legal Definitions of Sexual Assault

Hindrances to the normalization of the crime become especially apparent when we examine more closely the discrepancy between the law's articulation of what constitutes sexual assault and the definitions officials use in the warrant-issuing process. Law reformers in Michigan hoped that the statute would accomplish symbolic change by shifting the perspectives of members of the criminal justice system toward a view of criminal sexual assault encompassing more kinds of assaultive behavior. But when we presented respondents with two hypothetical cases now covered under Michigan's CSC statute, they indicated an adherence to a simple dichotomy between "real rape" and other sex crimes.[8]

Data from the Detroit Police Sex Crimes Unit show that there are fewer arrests for CSC4 cases than for other degrees of CSC, and this is probably because the criminal justice system tends to discount these reports. Their responses to hypothetical cases strongly point to the likelihood that police often will not investigate a case if the complainant has a previous sexual history with her assailant. And while sex past is also important to the prosecutor's decision for that group, a "legitimate" case must also include threats or evidence of violence.

In order to achieve some measure of their definitions of appropriate (as opposed to criminal) sexual behavior, respondents were presented with two scenarios portraying typical "marginal" cases. The first depicts the rape of a girl by her boyfriend on a date; the second involves the sexual harassment of a secretary by her employer. Each scenario has four versions; with each successive version, the assault becomes more flagrant. Circumstances that contribute to the marginal nature of the case—that is, the fact that the man and woman had both been drinking or that they had had a prior sexual relationship—were systematically eliminated as respondents proceeded through additional versions of the scenarios. In the fourth version, the offenses described are most serious. In the date scenario the element of force resulting in physical trauma is added; in the office scenario coercion in the form of the threat of loss of employment is added. In none of the four versions of either scenario does the woman actually consent to the man's sexual advances, although some versions include evidence that has been used traditionally to prove consent. According to the law, all four versions of both scenarios portray behaviors that are criminal. Table 6–7 displays elements included in both scenarios; complete scenarios are contained in the questionnaire in Appendix B.

All respondents were asked to speculate about the case-processing decisions they might make in successive versions of each of these hypothetical situations. Specifically, police were asked if they would be likely to seek a warrant; prosecutors were asked if they would issue one and, if a warrant were issued, what the

Table 6–7  Elements Included in Date and Office Scenarios

| Version | Date Context | Office Context |
|---|---|---|
| 1 | Previous sexual relationship<br>Presence of alcohol<br>Low level of force | Previous sexual relationship<br>Presence of alcohol<br>Low level of coercion |
| 2 | Previous sexual relationship<br>No alcohol<br>Low level of force | No previous sexual relationship<br>Presence of alcohol<br>Low level of coercion |
| 3 | No previous sexual relationship<br>No alcohol<br>Low level of force | No previous sexual relationship<br>No alcohol<br>Low level of coercion |
| 4 | No previous sexual relationship<br>No alcohol<br>High level of force | No previous sexual relationship<br>No alcohol<br>High level of coercion |

charge would be. Finally, we asked all respondents whether, in their opinion, a jury would be likely to convict.[9]

Although all of the respondents had doubtlessly encountered similar cases, it is important to emphasize that they were responding to hypothetical situations. Their responses indicate agreement or lack of agreement with the law's definition of criminal sexual assault and cannot necessarily be extrapolated to their behavior. As the social psychological literature documents, behavioral intentions and actual behavior are not one and the same. Furthermore, the "demand" characteristics of the interview were likely to induce at least some respondents to give what would be perceived as socially desirable, rather than accurate, responses. If anything, they may have exaggerated their actual agreement with the law's definition of criminal actions.

## Police Definition of the Crime

The police responses to the scenarios indicate that the sexual relationship between the complainant and the accused is a crucial determinant of whether a warrant will be sought. Their responses show that in the first version of either scenario the victim would not fare very well: Her chances would be about 50–50 that the police officer would seek a warrant. Fifty-nine percent reported that they would seek a warrant in the first scenario, and 59 per-

Table 6–8  Police and Prosecutor Responses to Variations in Scenario Items

| Scenarios | Percentage of Police Who Would Seek Warrants, Police Self-Reports (N = 39) | Percentage of Prose-cutors Who Would Issue Warrants, Prosecutor Self-Reports (N = 40) |
|---|---|---|
| *Date Scenario* | | |
| 1. Past sex history and drinking | 59 | 10 |
| 2. Past sex history—*no* drinking | 59 | 10 |
| 3. *No* past sex history—*no* drinking | 85 | 58 |
| 4. *No* past sex history—*no* drinking and physical violence | 100 | 98 |
| *Office Scenario* | | |
| 1. Past sex history and drinking | 46 | 3 |
| 2. *No* past sex history—drinking | 82 | 18 |
| 3. *No* past sex history—*no* drinking | 90 | 70 |
| 4. *No* past sex history—*no* drinking and threats of loss of employment | 92 | 88 |

cent would in the second scenario. In the last version of each, however, in which elements of coercion or violence are present, nearly all officers said they would seek a warrant (see Table 6–8).

In the first scenario, which portrays a date, the existence of a previous sexual relationship is eliminated in the third version of the scenario and the percentage of police seeking warrants increases sharply from 59 percent to 85 percent. In the second scenario, involving sexual harassment, the sexual relationship is deleted in version two, and the percentage of police reporting that they would seek warrants again increases dramatically from 46 percent to 82 percent. In the fourth versions of both scenarios, almost every officer would seek a warrant. According to respondents, the other situational characteristics (drinking, the use of force, and coercion) are of much lesser consequence than is the victim's sexual history with her assailant.[10]

## Prosecutors' Definitions of the Crime

Prosecutors differ from police in some important ways. According to their self-reports (shown in Table 6–8), prosecutors are less likely than police to take action in these cases. Further, prosecutors place less importance upon the victim's previous sexual relationship with her assailant. Ten percent reported that they would issue a warrant if presented with the circumstances described in the first version of the date scenario, while 3 percent would issue warrants in the first version of the sexual harassment scenario. In the date scenario, the existence of a previous sexual relationship is important. When we eliminated it in version three, the number of prosecutors reporting that they would issue warrants increased from 10 percent to 58 percent. Still, this means that only half the prosecutors would pursue such a case, as compared with 85 percent of the police. As one prosecutor explained, "Petting implies consent." All but one prosecutor would issue a warrant in the fourth version of the date scenario, where there is evidence of force and coercion. In general, prosecutors report that a demonstrable level of violence is a persuasive prerequisite to the pursuit of a case.

The difference between prosecutors and police officers is even more pronounced in the office scenario. Whereas the elimination of a past sexual relationship between the secretary and her employer is the key factor for the police, for the prosecutors this is of little consequence; only six additional prosecutors (an increase of 15 percent) would be persuaded to act by this change. Only when the offense occurs as the secretary is working late as a favor to her boss, rather than following an office party where she had been drinking and "flirting," would a majority (70 percent) of prosecutors issue a warrant.

These findings indicate that the victim's behavior and personal characteristics as much as the defendant's are scrutinized and judged, and the victim's sexual history in particular continues to influence the decisions police and prosecutors make. The evidence suggests that if a victim has ever been receptive to the assailant's sexual advances—from "flirting" with him to having consensual intercourse with him in the past—then officials will be likely to discount her report. Where the law does not specifically spell out actions criminal justice officials may take, its symbolic impact, if any, is minimal. Where the law's definition of criminally assaultive behavior differs from that of officials, its capacity to counteract personal discretion is limited. The result is that "marginal cases" are not easily introduced into the system.

Stereotypes and attitudes about the victim's culpability in sexual assault continue to play a role in CSC case processing.[11] And the system itself is cumbersome and complex; any change—whether welcomed or not—that does not radically restructure it seems quickly diluted and defused. When ingrained attitudes and organizational constraints are combined, "business as usual" prevails. The degree of CSC with which the assailant is charged is an indication of the prosecutor's perception of the seriousness of the offense, combined with expectations about the plea-bargaining process. Michigan's statute clearly spells out circumstances falling under each of the four degrees of CSC. The man's behavior described in version four of the date scenarios is technically criminal sexual conduct in the first degree, punishable by up to twenty-five years in prison. Almost all of the prosecutors (thirty-nine out of forty) state that they would issue a warrant in this last version; however, half (49 percent) would issue warrants for CSC3 and two would issue warrants for assault, a misdemeanor with a maximum two-year sentence.

In version four of the office scenario, the employer could technically be charged at least with CSC4 and probably with second-degree criminal sexual conduct. Only one prosecutor, however, said that he would issue a warrant for CSC2. Most would issue warrants at CSC4, but four would charge assault and one said the employer should be charged with a civil rights infringement. None specifically mentioned avenues of recourse available through new sexual harassment legislation.

These data are especially surprising in light of the common assumption that prosecutors "charge high" in order to gain leverage in the plea-bargaining process. Prosecutors in this instance are certainly not inflating the charge; on the contrary, the self-reports indicate that the majority may undercharge. Because prosecutors demonstrate familiarity with the law's provisions, their reported propensity to undercharge is probably not due to ignorance. Especially in the date scenario, it seems more likely that they are unwilling to bring the full weight of the law and the sanctions of the criminal justice system to bear on such an assault. They may underestimate the seriousness of the case described and, to the extent that this amount to failure to recognize the assaultive nature of the incident, the law's impact can be questioned.

## Prosecutors and Winnability

For prosecutors the ability to win cases is the primary measure of their competence. Their superiors evaluate their performance based on win/loss records, and—for the politically ambitious—so does the community at large. When deciding whether to try a case, prosecutors are therefore concerned with its winnability—that is, their assessment of the chance that they will achieve a conviction. Their decision reflects their perception of a judge's or jury's response to a case. Even now, as prosecutors mentioned over and over again, sexual assaults are among the most difficult cases to try. Because it is not in their best interests to pursue unwinnable cases, prosecutors' preoccupation with conviction rates prevents marginal CSC cases from entering the criminal justice system.

The scenarios amplify some of the ways in which a case's characteristics can affect its winnability. The data also support the inference that the early versions of these scenarios depict cases that prosecutors do not consider winnable. The few who said that they would issue warrants in either versions one or two of the scenarios do not expect to obtain convictions. As the proportion of prosecutors issuing warrants increases, however, so does the proportion who believe that the cases can be won. Among the thirty-nine prosecutors who reported that they would issue warrants in the fourth version of the date scenario, only four believed that they could not win the case. And, responding to the fourth version of the office scenario, only five prosecutors who would pursue the case believed that a jury would not convict. Most will not issue warrants unless they expect to get a conviction; few seem to be given to symbolic gestures.

A prosecutor's assessment of a case's winnability is a gauge of more than an individual's ambitions or attitudes; it is also probably a fairly accurate reflection of community attitudes toward and tolerance for expanded definitions of sexual assault. The statute improved prosecutors' chances for convictions generally. But prosecutors, at least, do not believe that marginal cases will fare well with juries, the group that provides the interface between law and society. As one prosecutor concluded, "The CSC statute has enlarged the scope of activities that are considered criminal. But the community has not equally enlarged its sense of what is criminal. The statute still precedes the senses of society."

## Summary

The criminal sexual conduct statute has contributed to increases in convictions and arrests, apparently while improving the victim's experience. But disturbing discontinuities regarding the approach to CSC complaints appeared in interviews with officials and with crisis center staff, the people who most consistently monitor the performance of the criminal justice system. The majority of those we interviewed said that they handled CSC cases much as they would other equally serious crimes, but an important minority dissented. The latter cited a belief in fabrications or emphasized features of the complainant's character or behavior as support for their skeptical approach. Some respondents thought that, while the stereotypical rape was the most heinous of crimes and should be punished accordingly, a date rape was a risk a woman brings upon herself if she goes to a bar alone. Others believed rape is easily charged and therefore deserving of rigorous investigation to protect males from false accusation. These prejudices mean that an individual who endorses the law wholeheartedly and has nothing but empathy for most victims may still sometimes focus the case investigation on the victim's behavior or character.

Like any law, the CSC statute guarantees neither its own application nor—even if applied—convictions for charged assailants. Our continuing concern about the law and the criminal justice system centers on professional discretion, which the law did not attempt to modify directly. Those unwritten rules guide invisible decisions—decisions that are still influenced by mistrust of rape victims and a concern among prosecutors with winning cases.

## Endnotes

1. Those who noted a change in their jurisdictions said that the unfounding rate had increased—that is, that a lower percentage of sexual assault reports were now pursued. Some suggested that the women's movement and publicity about the law had contributed to more reports of "marginal" cases that the police are less likely to pursue. One police officer said, "Because of the new law, we have people reporting things that aren't a crime. It's harder to explain that these cases don't fall under the new law." As an example, he cited a case he had turned away in

which the complainant had been sexually assaulted by her boyfriend. But the new law *does* cover such assaults.

2. Only 25 percent indicated that rape reports were more often unfounded. Forty percent said the unfounding rate was actually higher in other crimes; 35 percent thought the rates were about equal.

3. President's Commission on Law Enforcement and the Administration of Justice, *The Challenge of Crime in a Free Society* (Washington, D.C.: U.S. Government Printing Office, 1967); National Commission on the Causes and Prevention of Violence, *To Establish Justice and to Ensure Domestic Tranquility* (1969); National Institute for Law Enforcement and Criminal Justice, LEAA, *Forcible Rape: A National Survey of the Response by Prosecutors*, Vol. 1 (March 1977).

4. Interdepartmental differences account for some of the reasons for unfoundings. One study (Note, Police Discretion, 1968) found that unfounded complaints involve the following factors: (1) delay in reporting by victim, (2) lack of physical evidence supporting the complaint, (3) refusal by victim to submit to a medical examination, and (4) previous relationship between victim and offender. Among the other factors that lead to unfoundings are police officers' failure to apprehend the suspect or the victim's refusal to prosecute. Most of these factors are not relevant to whether or not a crime has occurred; they pertain to whether or not a conviction can be achieved—that is, the "winnability" of the case.

5. On the whole, respondents report few false reports. Ninety percent of judges, prosecutors, and crisis center staff members interviewed believe that less than one in five sexual assault complaints is fabricated. Two-thirds or more of defense attorneys and police concur with this estimate.

6. National Institute for Law Enforcement and Criminal Justice (1977), *op. cit.*

7. Although their anecdotes deal with female victims, it is not possible to determine whether the skepticism of some respondents derives from a mistrust of women or of rape victims regardless of their sex.

8. For a comprehensive review of the validity and reliability of vignettes in studies of rape, see Linda B. Bourque and Rita Engelhardt, "Designing Vignettes: A Review and Critique with Particular Reference to Studies of Rape," and "Defining Rape: Force, Race and Occupational Status as Predictors"; and Linda B. Bourque, "Reliability of Vignettes in Measuring Attitudes," unpublished manuscripts, School of Public Health, University of California (Los Angeles, 1981).

9. Defense attorneys, judges, and crisis center activists were also asked what they thought police and prosecutors would do if confronted with these cases, and police and prosecutors were asked to speculate about the other group's behavior.

10. The data reveal that most crisis center staff and judges believe that the police will seek warrants only in the fourth version of the scenarios, where force and/or coercion are present and the victim does not have a sexual history with the accused. This divergence of opinion is difficult to interpret. Crisis center staff and judges are merely observers of the war-

rant-issuing process and therefore may not have accurate knowledge of it. Based on the biased sample of cases they see, they may be exaggerating the unwillingness of police to pursue marginal cases. Prosecutors tend to agree with the police self-reports; nevertheless, the estimates given by judges and crisis center staff lead us to treat with caution the police self-reports and to speculate that they report themselves as behaving more consistently with the law than they actually do.

11. For a more complete analysis of the influence of attitudes and sexual assault stereotypes, see Jeanne C. Marsh, Nathan Caplan, Alison Giest, Gary Gregg, Janice Harrington, and Daniel Sharphorn, *Law Reform in the Prevention and Treatment of Rape,* Final Report to National Center for Prevention and Control of Rape, National Institute of Mental Health (July 1980).

*Chapter 7*

# UNDERSTANDING THE
# NATURE OF REFORM

At the time of the law's passage, the law reformers were a group of women concerned with the treatment of rape victims in the criminal justice system. They aligned themselves with lawmakers concerned with controlling crime and passed a law that was ahead of the thinking of much of the general public. Friedman (1967) suggests that it is at this point that the law has its greatest potential for impact—for initiating further social change:

> (F)resh law is a hybrid; half ratification, half real inducement to change. Formal legal change often comes at the middle point in a social process which requires a number of distinct steps for its completion. Formal legal change ratifies those steps already taken, but it forces or hurries society along with regard to the steps not yet taken (p. 363).

There was skepticism among the law reformers about whether the statute, once enacted, would be implemented. For that reason, its influence on reporting, arrest, and conviction rates was expected to be minimal. Most observers, including the law reformers themselves, were more sanguine with respect to the law's capacity to achieve symbolic goals. They argued that the visibility generated by the reform effort and the redefinition of the crime within the statute would initiate a process by which the concerns of rape victims as well as the women's movement would be legitimized. Beginning with changes in attitudes among criminal justice system officials, they expected the law to begin to change cultural norms surrounding rape. Our findings would seem to disprove both sets of expectations. The law had a measurable impact on crime statistics and was implemented by a system typically characterized as unlikely to do so. But the attitudes of people in the criminal justice system do not reflect a substantially modified view of the crime or of the role of women in society.

The effectiveness of Michigan's criminal sexual conduct law can be documented directly in terms of the tangible goals that have been achieved. Convictions for criminal sexual conduct in the first degree (formerly "forcible rape") have increased substantially as a function of the reformed law. Consistent with this finding, prosecutors' chances of achieving convictions have improved, according to respondents. They additionally reported that prosecutors are able to win more types of cases than they were in the past, suggesting that the law's protection extends to more groups of people.

The findings further reveal that the law in Michigan has been implemented in such a way that the procedures used in sexual assault cases are now in many ways similar to those used for other crimes. The results indicate, however, that many aspects of criminal justice processing are left undisturbed by the law. Although victims are more frequently able to pursue their cases without derisive and discourteous treatment within the criminal justice system, a number of respondents continue to be skeptical of women reporting sexual assaults and to pursue more readily the cases of "worthy" victims. This is supported by the finding that polygraphs are used more often in sexual assault cases than in equally serious crimes and by respondents' estimates that there are more fabrications in sexual assault reports. Further, defense attorneys continue to investigate and, when they can, to introduce information about a complainant's sexual history.

Respondents cited specific provisions of the law as responsible for the positive changes documented. Prosecutors' improved chances to win convictions seem to derive from shifts in the burden of proof resulting from prohibiting the use of sexual history evidence and eliminating the need to prove resistance and non-consent. The way in which the law structures the offense into degrees, with punishment commensurate with the seriousness of the crime, also improves the chances of conviction. This feature of the law provides police and prosecutors with specific guidelines

for investigating and charging decisions. Further, it allows prosecutors to plea-bargain down to a sex offense which reflects the
nature of the crime. Respondents believe that the gender neutral
language of the law and its increased capacity to protect those
with potentially prejudicial sexual histories also increases the
types of cases that have a chance for conviction. Respondents felt
that the victim's experience in the criminal justice system, while
still difficult, is less onerous than it was in the past. The law's
limitation of sexual history evidence was overwhelmingly credited
with this improvement.

From the crime statistics as well as the perspective of those
who implement the law, then, there is considerable evidence that
the law has achieved the goal of exerting some control on decision
makers in the criminal justice system. It has also succeeded in
bringing the legal standards for cases more in line with those used
for other violent crimes reducing the trauma victims have traditionally suffered while prosecuting their assailants.

The evidence is more equivocal with regard to the law's capacity to constrain perceptions of the boundaries of sanctioned
behavior towards women. When respondents were asked about
the criminal nature of specific hypothetical situations designed to
reflect the expanded definition of sexual crimes contained in the
law, many—particularly prosecutors—seemed hesitant to pursue
cases having characteristics the law reformers specifically hoped
would be prosecuted under the new statute. The data revealed
that criminal justice officials have not yet assimilated the explicit
redefinition of rape contained in the new law's structure. Both
crime statistics and the interview data show that several respondents continue to adhere to a simple dichotomy between
"real rape" and other sex crimes. According to this perspective,
"real rape" is committed by sexual psychopaths who prey on
strangers. There is no argument about the relevance of the law
in these brutal cases. But the application of the law to other areas
of sexual conduct is considered, according to one respondent, to
be "messing with the folkways." (This respondent was clearly
referencing Sumner's often-stated dictum that "Stateways cannot
change Folkways.")

Overall, these findings were consistent across the six counties
studied, indicating that the CSC statute has had a pervasive effect
in Michigan regardless of the unique characteristics of different

regions or jurisdictions. This finding runs counter to the intuition that in rural counties, especially those lacking crisis centers, a law reform might be implemented to a lesser extent than in an urban area. The implementation and effectiveness of the statute do not seem to be dependent on jurisdictional factors.

## Determinants of the Law Reform's Effectiveness

The successful implementation of rape law reform has implications for diverse social programs and policies. Because so few reforms succeed, it has been difficult to develop a set of prescriptions that serve both the administrators of reforms and the advocates for change. Evaluations of program and policy implementation increasingly recognize the value of understanding organizations as channels or agents of change that determine effectiveness.[1] The usefulness of such evaluations depends also on their ability to enhance knowledge of the general conditions favorable to reform. A review of the success of Michigan's criminal sexual conduct statute reveals that it was determined by the characteristics of the law itself, the system implementing it, and the forces outside the system that pursued the change.

This study has focused on the interaction of the law and the criminal justice system. Let us now examine this interaction within the social context to refine our understanding of conditions conducive to reform. Specifically, we build on study findings to address the following questions: What exactly can we expect from a change in a rule of law? And what are the determinants, both within the criminal justice system and the social environment, of its impact? To address these questions, let us examine three clusters of variables: (1) the nature and specific provisions of the law, (2) the nature of the bureaucracy represented by the criminal justice system, and (3) the characteristics and continuing influence of social reform groups responsible for the enactment of the law as they continue to influence the organizational environment of the criminal justice system.

### Nature and Specific Provisions of the Law

As the functions of law became more clearly delineated, it is possible to more realistically anticipate potential effects.[2] Like most criminal laws, the criminal sexual conduct statute had as its purpose the redefinition of the crime and its victims, as well as appropriate punishments for those convicted. The law included several procedural changes designed to bring the handling of sexual assault crimes more in line with that of other violent crimes. And the results document the capacity for procedural changes to modify the processing of sexual assault laws by reducing discretion required in making certain decisions.

Laws that, like the criminal sexual conduct statute, specify the formal procedures through which cases must be processed have the best chance to influence the criminal justice system. For example, law-mandated preliminary hearings and grand jury or other routine court appearances are more likely to be complied with, if only in a *pro forma* manner. In some jurisdictions, preliminary hearings are convened but serve as a mechanism for plea-bargaining rather than as a means for determining probable cause.[3] The greater likelihood of compliance with laws that change procedures no doubt results from the fact that they are technically simple and easily monitored, characteristics that increase the implementability of any law reform.[4] In addition to successfully modifying procedures, laws can also have a powerful influence on the way in which jury trials are conducted. This is in part due to the monitoring function of a potential appeal.[5] It is also due to the tradition of the court. While all case processing leading up to the trial is characterized by cooperation and informal norms, the trial itself is characterized by formal procedures designed to reveal the strength of facts and to prove guilt or innocence.

The procedures outlined in the rape law focused primarily on trial proceedings. The degree structure clarified the evidence needed to convict for each charge of criminal sexual conduct and other provisions specifically prohibited evidence related to the victim's sex past. Officials adhered to these rules because, while for the reformers they were a means to improve the victim's experience, for the system they were a means to speed case processing and improve conviction and arrest records with reduced effort.

The law established rules and norms to replace discretion. Respondents concluded that, as a result, the law "normalized" the treatment of the crime. The procedures used in sexual assault cases are now, in many ways, similar to those used for other crimes. There are still instances in which the "normalization" of the crime is neither uniform nor complete. But the law's success in this regard reveals its capacity to exert control on decision making. Because the law specified so clearly the nature of an offense, the groups covered by the law, and the evidence that could be used as proof, it provided considerably more guidance in the processing of these cases than had been available before. Police and prosecutors describe the charging and warrant-issuing decisions as much easier under the law's guidelines, which clarify the behavior constituting the crime. The law also narrows the range of judicial discretion that needs to be exercised. Careful definition of the crime and establishment of procedures to be used in processing cases place limits on discretion and increase adherence to the law's intent.

Rape law reforms have been faulted for focusing on procedural changes related to the conduct of trial in that more than three-quarters of these cases never reach trial.[6] This is a legitimate concern, but the criticism ignores the evidence that laws can have only a minimal impact outside the courtroom; most research suggests that laws have little or no influence on the routine day-to-day practices of the criminal justice system.[7] Our findings support this assertion. For instance, warrant issuance and polygraph use remain untouched by law. Obviously, extrajudicial procedures which continue to single out rape victims for difficult treatment need to be addressed by other strategies. The initiation of a class action suit to restrain polygraph use in Detroit, discussed in the next section, provides a good example of an effective alternative.

*Awareness of the Law's Provisions.* More than one legal reform has failed simply because the individuals responsible for implementing it have no knowledge of the reform.[8] Familiarity with the law's options and intent among judges, attorneys, and crisis center staff in Michigan was impressive. While some respondents were uncertain about some of its aspects, most had detailed working knowledge of the law and its provisions.

The law reformers describe Michigan's criminal sexual conduct law as "a wrenching change from the past."[9] Early opponents of the law reform anticipated problems with dissemination of the legal changes to relevant public officials. They saw the law as too complex, technical, and awkwardly worded to be understood and implemented. In retrospect, however, respondents cited the scope and complexity of the law as one reason for its effective implementation. As one judge described it,

*The law was so different from the previous statute, it was so much more comprehensive and complex that it required a total administrative change. It became important for every person in the system to attend seminars and training sessions to determine what the new law would mean for him or her.*

Workshops for police, conducted by people both within and outside of sheriff's offices and police departments, provided technical information about the law's application. They increased the professionalism of those who handle sexual assault cases as well as focused attention on the crime, often creating an opportunity for crisis center workers and police to discuss options for cooperation.

Since the provisions were so progressive compared with the old statute and compared with those in almost any other state, the reform effort received a great deal of publicity. The early attention from the media provided an important channel of communication to criminal justice system officials as well as to the general public. Additionally, when the legislature was considering the bill, prominent prosecuting attorneys in Michigan saw the change as potentially problematic for them and became involved with drafting the language of some of the provisions. Because a critical group of individuals involved with the law on a daily basis developed a personal stake in it, they helped to insure its visibility.

Although the law's impact was felt primarily in the courtroom, leaving extrajudicial problems to be addressed by other reform strategies, most respondents felt the law had fulfilled its intent of improving victim experience and increasing successful prosecution. Provisions of the law had successfully capitalized on the characteristics of the criminal justice system to accomplish goals of the reform.

## Nature of the Criminal Justice Bureaucracy[10]

Naïveté about the nature of the criminal justice system and principles of organizational change serve as major obstacles to successful reform: As Raymond T. Nimmer says:[11]

*Since reforms differ in substance, in planning and development, the explanations for specific reform failures are diverse. In general,*

*however, the repetition of failure can be attributed in large part
to recurring misperceptions about the nature of the judicial process
and about how behavior within the process can be modified.*

Analysts of both organizational change and legal reform indicate
that the structural and functional characteristics of the criminal
justice system provide the organizational context in which change
occurs and are, therefore, crucial to the achievement of the reform's goals.[12]

*Structural Characteristics.*   The centralization, complexity, and
formalization of an organization are related to its capacity for
change or innovation, such as the implementation of a law reform.
It should be noted that structural characteristics related to pro-
posing and conceiving of change are typically opposite to those
related to the effective implementation of change.

The extent of centralization of an organization refers to the distribution of decision-making powers. The greater the hierarchy of
authority and the less the participation in decision making, the
greater the centralization. The criminal justice system has both a
centralized and decentralized power distribution—centralized because significant decision-making power clearly rests with the
chief prosecutor, and decentralized because of the highly spe-
cialized nonroutine tasks performed by others in the system. Both
the chief and assistant prosecutors, police officials, and judges
must make numerous autonomous decisions recurrently. Monitoring and coordinating them is difficult.

In this particular power structure, change is dependent on the
support and enthusiasm of the central decision maker, so the
policies and influence of the chief prosecutor will affect implementation. Either by force of personality or establishment of
structural change (such as special investigative units), the central
authority can direct organizational attention or resources toward
compliance with the change. But the chief prosecutor's authority
must be considered in conjunction with his or her limited capacity
to monitor the behavior of lower-level personnel. The chief prosecutor's tenure depends on both performance and political position; that of lower-level personnel does not.

The degree of complexity in an organization refers to the diversity of occupations and the level of professionalism. High diversity
and professionalism in organizations typically results in the initiation of more changes but the implementation of fewer. This

characteristic of the criminal justice system, whose numerous occupational specialities are highly professionalized, has critical implications for change. While the organization might generate a
large number of ideas for reform, few would take effect unless
promoted by a centralized authority like the chief prosecutor.

Formalization, or the emphasis an organization places on following specific rules and procedures, is assumed to interfere with
the identification of the need for change. In theory, formal rules
allocate power among participants in the criminal justice system.
For example, judges control sentence decisions and prosecutors
control charging decisions; defense attorneys control selection of
issues to be raised and police officers control the availability of
information and evidence.

In practice, however, informal rules readjust these relationships. Implicit permission, demands, and the expectations of others
influence individual behavior. The frequent use of discretionary
decision making translates the formal rules into informal practice.
Discretionary decisions are made in anticipation of the behavior
of others in the system. Theory predicts that within such an informal situation the need for change would be easily recognized
but difficult to implement. Because change requires deviation
from informal norms with uncertain consequences, it is difficult
to bring about a situation with highly functional, entrenched informal rules and procedures.

*Functional Characteristics.* The criminal justice system, like
every other organization, seeks first and foremost to maintain itself. With a large number of cases and high demand for case
disposition, efficient case processing is the dominant motivation
of most individuals. Statutes, case law, and administrative policies
determine the boundaries of criminal justice procedure. Again,
however, informal norms and expectations determine the outcome
of a case, and these are shaped primarily by the desire—shared
by all participants—to process cases as quickly as possible.

In many ways, the second motivating characteristic of participants in the criminal justice system, the acquisition of power,
is related to the first: The more power an individual acquires, the
more cooperation he or she can expect from others and the more
efficiently cases can be processed. Whenever a reform mandates,
permits, or suggests a means for officials within the organization
to expand their sphere of influence, the reform is more likely to

be implemented. An expanded sphere of influence could be in the form of career advancement, control over more financial resources, more staff, or more public attention.

Essentially, then, the decentralized, highly complex, and informal structure of the criminal justice system is not conducive to implementing change. But its functional characteristics can be exploited to counteract bureaucratic inertia. The capacity for change derives from the ability of the law, the law reformers, or both, to appeal to the primary interests of the participants in the criminal justice system—that is, to minimize time and resources and to maximize individual power and prestige. The implementation of the criminal sexual conduct statute was furthered to the extent that the law and its advocates were responsive to these characteristics of the system.

There were several ways in which the law addressed criminal justice participants' need to cope with overwhelming caseloads. The study results show that once officials in the criminal justice system became familiar with the law, their jobs became easier and they were able to perform them more efficiently. For police officers, the law specified evidence required for each sexual assault and contributed to a more straightforward investigation procedure. It gave prosecutors specific guidelines for charging decisions and increased the likelihood of achieving convictions through plea-bargaining or through trial.

When new legislation allows officials to increase their power and prestige, the legislation is more likely to be implemented. When Michigan's criminal sexual conduct law was enacted, several prosecutors responded to the increased legitimacy the law brought to the crime by setting up special prosecutorial units to speed and consolidate sexual assault case processing. In some jurisdictions, the unit was collapsed with existing select units designed to handle the most serious cases, such as repeat offenders. In other jurisdictions, the special unit retained its own social worker or crisis counselor to aid the victim and in turn the prosecutor. Respondents in every county said that these special units attracted the most able and ambitious prosecutors and could be used to demonstrate the concern and sensitivity of the chief prosecutor with respect to this crime. Since the law additionally made it easier for prosecutors to achieve convictions, a central criterion for career advancement among prosecutors, in many counties the law served as a mechanism for expanding prosecutorial power and influence.

Thus, consistent with emerging evidence regarding legal changes, the Michigan law reform resulted in some important procedural reforms and had a less obvious impact on attitudes about the definition of the crime. The capacity of the law to influence these changes at all appeared to be in part a function of the law's capacity to facilitate more efficient case processing and expansion of influence among criminal justice personnel. But the law did not merely interact with the system; the interest groups who brought and maintained pressure for change served as important catalysts for sustaining the reaction.

## Influence of the Law Reformers: The Organizational Environment

The initiation or adoption of change depends on the degree to which an organization is accountable to outside groups, whether for funds, political support, or clients. For many criminal justice officials, accountability takes the form of responsibility to those who elect them.

Ideally, if constituencies are to succeed, they must design reforms whose costs to the organization do not outweigh benefits; they must establish and maintain legitimacy; and finally, because the enactment of a law and its implementation are two different matters, they must remain organized and committed long enough to monitor and augment the system's compliance with the reform.

The implementation of the criminal sexual conduct law sets up a situation in which costs of implementation and change are concentrated in the criminal justice system, while the benefits are dispersed to the population of potential victims. Wilson and Handler argue that in such situations opposition to the change tends to be intense and, because there are no tangible benefits to those pushing for change, it is often difficult for those groups to organize and remain organized.[13] The law reformers have been able to overcome these problems for two reasons.

First, because the law is compatible with the interests of criminal justice officials, the difficulties it initially seemed to present were neutralized or converted into assets. A new constituency to promote implementation has emerged within the system precisely because the early effects of the law benefitted many officials. Maintaining the status quo now means preserving the salutory effects of the law both structurally, through continuation of highly professionalized sexual assault units, and functionally, by preserving the efficiency the law lends to case processing. Furthermore, a growing number of criminal justice officials, from elected chief prosecutors to police detectives, have established reputations for themselves or their units by promoting the law. The importance of female police officers in particular has been demonstrated; many women in the police force have been able to establish and have their competence recognized by administering change in sexual assault case processing.

Second, the nature of the coalition formed to revise Michigan's rape law has contributed both to its legitimacy and its capacity to sustain activity. Members of the Michigan Task Force on Rape achieved crucial support for the law by aligning themselves with conservative legislators and other law-and-order advocates. It is partly because this coalition was possible that rape law reform became a target of the movement. Subsequent to the law's passage, coalitions of diverse groups have formed in response to particular events, such as a controversial case or the policy of a detective unit or prosecutor's office. This has kept the issue before the public and exerted pressure on the criminal justice system.

Wilson has pointed out that it is not unusual for laws to be enacted as a result of temporary coalitions supported by dramatic historical events and the media.[14] Once the law has been enacted, there is likely to be substantial disagreement among the groups within the coalition with respect to procedures appropriate for carrying out the law; implementation has much less visibility and much less media appeal.

As previously noted, law reforms like the criminal sexual conduct statute have been criticized because they do not address many aspects of case processing that take place outside the courtroom. These "gaps" in the law's coverage have meant that abuse of victims still occurs in the criminal justice system, and, when it does, community response has followed. For instance, as mentioned previously the Women's Justice Center in Detroit initiated a class action suit against the Detroit Police Department for its routine use of polygraphs with rape victims. Because the plaintiffs in the case were black, prominent members of Detroit's black community became part of the coalition that mobilized to publicize the case and the issues behind it. At a police commissioners' hearing on the policy, the picket line included two Detroit city council members. The suit was eventually dropped, but polygraph use has been stopped by state legislation which prohibits law-enforcement officials or prosecutors from requesting or requiring rape victims to take these lie-detector tests. The criminal sexual conduct statute's incomplete coverage may actually have forced community involvement in this instance. Thus, coalitions have changed and remained vital to address the issues the law did not.

Advocates, meanwhile, have specifically monitored the implementation of the statute. Crisis center counselors are often present at court as victim advocates. They not only offer support to victims but can observe the extent of compliance or noncompliance with the law. Because counselors may begin involvement with a victim at the emergency room immediately after the assault, they may follow the case through all stages of processing by the system. Their presence alone may assure more careful attention by officials to the letter and intent of the law.

While protecting victims' rights, crisis centers have typically pursued styles either of cooperation or confrontation with the system, but the two are often combined. In one community, a crisis center directly confronted a prosecutor's policy of "charging low" in sexual assault cases. The center posted security for costs to force the prosecutor to charge CSC1, not CSC3. In another community, a crisis center director has determined that it is important to establish legitimacy with law-enforcement officials, so the center primarily tries to cooperate with investigation. Over time, the chief detective has found center assistance invaluable because victims who have received some counseling make better witnesses on the stand. As a matter of routine, he now contacts the center whenever a rape complaint is brought. As the center director put it, "We can't rock the boat until we're in it."

The incidence of rape nationwide keeps it in the news. The grisly details of a brutal rape have always drawn media attention, but informed by the women's movement, this attention now takes a different character. And our respondents were acutely aware of it. As one police officer said, "We live and die by the press."

It remains unclear how long and how intense this monitoring must be to overcome the natural resistance of criminal justice organizations to changes required by law. Downs, and Strickland and Johnson[15] describe the ebb and flow of concern about particular social issues in terms of the "issue-attention cycle." This view describes a tendency for social reform groups to, if not lose interest in particular issues, turn their attention to other related concerns. This tendency is problematic when pressure from these groups is such a crucial ingredient in the implementation of the reform.

## The Limits of Law Reform

What can we expect from a legal reform? Study findings indicate that a law's success depends on the interplay among a constellation of factors related to the law, the system, and the involvement of social reform groups promoting change. Law has its most profound influence on simple, straightforward procedures in which compliance is easy to monitor. Its capacity to change routine functioning of the criminal justice system is minimal except to the extent that it facilitates case processing and enhances the power of participants. When social reform groups maintain pressure by monitoring system performance, they enhance accountability by creating opportunities for participants to reap the benefits of positive public attention.

Thus, Michigan's criminal sexual conduct law improved victim experience and influenced convictions primarily, our respondents believed, by altering trial procedures related to admissible evidence. However, it is not clear that these procedural changes alone could have been effective. The comprehensiveness of the reform in Michigan and the "wrenching change" it required in administrative procedures was considered necessary to force attention on the issues addressed by and specific provisions of the law. The clear redefinition of the crime and of its potential victims provided guidelines that streamlined case processing and brought more types of cases into the criminal justice system. But procedural changes do not appear to generalize beyond those clearly specified by the law. And in some cases, such as the use of *in-camera* hearings, clearly specified provisions may be ignored. Participants implement most provisions while maintaining attitudes essentially inconsistent with the law's intent. Attitudes of these officials may change in time, but attitude change is clearly not a short-term effect of the law. The extent of the law's implementation was clearly enhanced by pressure exerted from groups external to the criminal justice system. In Michigan these groups increased implementation as well as promoted changes beyond the influence of the law itself. The handling of rape cases in arenas outside the judicial system remain necessary targets for reform.

Law reform represents one of many strategies that have been employed to address the problem of rape. An assessment of the nature of changes possible through this strategy enables a better articulation of the multiple responses necessary to meet the long-term goals of reformers. This assessment validates the importance of law reform efforts that are taking place in most states but it underscores the critical importance of other strategies as well, including victim assistance programs, distribution of rape evidence collection kits, injunctions preventing the use of polygraphs with rape victims, hot lines, speak-outs, and demonstrations.[16] Michigan's criminal sexual conduct law was clearly a necessary condition for the progress that has been made, but far from a sufficient one.

## Endnotes

1. Edwin Hargrove, *The Missing Link* (Washington, D.C.: The Urban Institute, 1975) and Sara S. McLanahan, "Organizational Issues in U.S. Health Policy Implementation: Participation, Discretion, and Accountability," *The Journal of Applied Behavioral Science* (1980), 16 (3), pp. 354–369.
2. Malcolm Feeley, "The Concept of Laws in Social Science: A Critique and Notes on an Expanded View," *Law and Society Review* (1976), 3, pp. 407–425.
3. Nimmer cites the example of Donald M. McIntyre, "A Study of Judicial Dominance of the Charging Process," *J. Criminal L.C. and P.S.* (1968), 59, p. 463.
4. Handler, *op. cit.*
5. Nimmer, *op. cit.*, p. 33.
6. Leigh Bienen, "Rape III—National Developments in Rape Reform Legislation," *Women's Rights Law Reporter* (1980), 6 (3), pp. 179–213.
7. Nimmer, *op. cit.*, p. 32.
8. John Robertson and P. Teitelbaum, "Optimizing Legal Impact: A Case Study in Search of a Theory," *Wisconsin Law Review* (1973), pp. 665–

726; R.J. Mendalie, L. Zeitz, and P. Alexander, "Custodial Police In-
terrogation in Our Nation's Capital: The Attempt to Implement Mir-
anda," *Michigan Law Review* (1968), pp. 1362–1374; Norman Lefsten,
V. Stapleton, and L. Teitelbaum, "In Search of Juvenile Justice: Gault
and Its Implementation," *Law and Society Review* (1969), p. 491.

9. Virginia B. Nordby, "Legal Effects of Proposed Rape Reform Bills,"
   mimeograph (April 1974).

10. Frank Remington and Donald J. Newman, *The Administration of Crim-
    inal Justice* (Chicago: American Bar Foundation, 1962), describe the
    criminal justice system as a complex organization that includes major
    decision-making sources in the legislature, courts, and administrative
    agencies (police, prosecutor, and corrections). Our discussion of the
    criminal justice bureaucracy is consistent with this definition.

11. Raymond T. Nimmer, *The Nature of System Change: Reform Impact
    in the Criminal Courts* (Chicago: The American Bar Foundation, 1978),
    p. 2.

12. Everett M. Rogers and Rekha Agarwall-Rogers, *Communication in
    Organizations* (New York: The Free Press, 1976); Jerald Hage and
    Michael Aiken, *Social Change in Complex Organizations* (New York:
    Random House, 1970); Mayer N. Zald, "On the Social Control of In-
    dustries," *Social Forces* (1978), 57, pp. 79–101; John D. McCarthy and
    Mayer N. Zald, "Resource Mobilization and Social Movements: A Partial
    Theory," *American Journal of Sociology* (1977), 82, pp. 1212–1241; and
    Mayer N. Zald, "Political Economy: A Framework for Comparative
    Analysis," in Mayer Zald, *Power in Organizations* (Nashville: Vander-
    bilt University Press, 1970); and Katherine S. Teilman, "A Theory to
    Predict the Implementation of Reform Legislation," University of South-
    ern California, unpublished manuscript.

13. See James Q. Wilson, "The Politics of Regulation," in J.W. McKie
    (ed.), *Social Responsibility and the Business Predicament* (Washington,
    D.C.: Brookings Institution, 1974), pp. 135–168, for a cogent discussion
    of the impact of the distribution of costs and benefits on potential for
    policy implementation; Joel F. Handler, *Social Movements and the Legal
    System: A Theory of Law Reform and Social Change* (New York:
    Academic Press, 1978).

14. Wilson, *op. cit.*

15. Anthony Downs, "Up and Down with Ecology—the Issue Attention
    Cycle," *Public Interest* (1972), 28 (Summer), pp. 38–50; D.A. Strick-
    land and A.F. Johnston, "Issue Elasticity in Political Systems," *Journal
    of Political Economy* (1970), p. 78 (September/October), pp. 1069–92.

16. For a more detailed discussion of potential strategies, see Jeanne C.
    Marsh, Nathan Caplan, Alison Geist, Gary Gregg, Janice Harrington,
    and Daniel Sharphorn, *Law Reform in the Prevention and Treatment
    of Rape*, Final Report to National Center for Prevention and Control of
    Rape, National Institute of Mental Health (July 1980).

*Appendix A*

# THE QUESTIONNAIRE

Unique questionnaires were prepared for each group of respondents according to their occupational roles. The instrument used for prosecutors was the most exhaustive, and the others were patterned upon it. Thus the prosecutor questionnaire is included here as the most representative.

● Interviewer name _____

● County_____

● Office_____

● Date_____

● Length of Interview_____
                                (Minutes)

    Before we begin the interview, I would like briefly to explain the nature of the study.  We are trying to determine possible effects of Michigan's Criminal Sexual Conduct law. Because of your experience in the criminal justice system, we are interested in your own opinions and insights that pertain to the law.

    The interview usually takes about one and a half hours. Your anonymity will be protected, and your answers will be treated confidentially.

I have your official title as

● _____

● Age    _____

● Sex    _____

● Race   _____

Part I

INTERVIEWER:  IF RESPONDENT HAS NO PRE-CSC LAW EXPERIENCE, CHECK HERE [ ]
            ——→   GO TO 2a.


1.   In your opinion, what are the three most significant changes brought
     about by Michigan's new CSC law?

     _____

     _____

     _____

     _____

     _____

     _____

     _____


2a.  Approximately what percent of CSC reports received by police in your
     jurisdiction reach the prosecutor for a warrant decision?  _____


INTERVIEWER CHECKPOINT

[ ]   IF LESS THAN 100%, ASK 2b.

 ↓    [ ]   IF 100% or DK ——→   GO TO 3a.


2b.  Why do you think some reports fail to reach your office?

     _____

     _____

     _____

     _____

     _____

3a. How often do you or the police ask the complainant to take a polygraph in a CSC case?

All cases      Most cases      Some cases      Few cases      Never      DK
[ ]              [ ]              [ ]              [ ]          [ ]        [ ]

3b. How often do you or the police ask the complainant to take a polygraph in the case of another equally serious crime?

All cases      Most cases      Some cases      Few cases      Never      DK
[ ]              [ ]              [ ]              [ ]          [ ]        [ ]


INTERVIEWER CHECKPOINT

[ ] IF 3a AND 3b ARE DIFFERENT, ASK 3c.

[ ] IF 3a AND 3b ARE THE SAME OR DK ⟶ GO TO 4a.


3c. Could you please explain why there is this difference in the use of polygraphs?

_____

_____

_____

_____

_____

_____

_____

_____

_____

_____

4a. Please turn to page 1 in your booklet. Now I'd like to ask you about factors which might lead you to <u>deny</u> warrants in CSC cases. Please refer to the list and check how <u>often</u> each of the following items contributes to the decision to <u>deny</u> a warrant in a CSC case:

|  | Always | Usually | Sometimes | Rarely | Never | DK |
|---|---|---|---|---|---|---|
| (1) No documented physical injury | | | | | | |
| (2) Lack of corroborating witness | | | | | | |
| (3) Lack of physical evidence | | | | | | |
| (4) Suspect has good alibi | | | | | | |
| (5) Victim withdraws complaint | | | | | | |
| (6) Lack of prompt complaint | | | | | | |
| (7) Problems with suspect identification | | | | | | |
| (8) Victim fails a polygraph | | | | | | |
| (9) Suspect passes polygraph | | | | | | |
| (10) Inconsistencies in complainant's story | | | | | | |
| (11) Poor personal credibility of complainant | | | | | | |
| (12) Offense not sufficiently serious | | | | | | |
| (13) Other (please specify): | | | | | | |
| (14) Other (please specify): | | | | | | |
| (15) Other (please specify): | | | | | | |

4b. Now turn to page 2. What about circumstances in which you deny warrants for other equally serious crimes? How often do the following contribute to that decision?

| | | Always | Usually | Sometimes | Rarely | Never | DK |
|---|---|---|---|---|---|---|---|
| (1) | No documented physical injury | | | | | | |
| (2) | Lack of corroborating witness | | | | | | |
| (3) | Lack of physical evidence | | | | | | |
| (4) | Suspect has good alibi | | | | | | |
| (5) | Victim withdraws complaint | | | | | | |
| (6) | Lack of prompt complaint | | | | | | |
| (7) | Problems with suspect identification | | | | | | |
| (8) | Victim fails a polygraph | | | | | | |
| (9) | Suspect passes polygraph | | | | | | |
| (10) | Inconsistencies in complainant's story | | | | | | |
| (11) | Poor personal credibility of complainant | | | | | | |
| (12) | Offense not sufficiently serious | | | | | | |
| (13) | Other (please specify): | | | | | | |
| (14) | Other (please specify): | | | | | | |
| (15) | Other (please specify): | | | | | | |

4c.  Of those that you have personally handled what percentage of CSC warrant requests have you denied? _____

4d.  How about equally serious crimes? _____

INTERVIEWER CHECKPOINT

```
[ ] IF 4c AND 4d ARE DIFFERENT, ASK 4e.

    [ ] IF 4c AND 4d ARE THE SAME ——→ GO TO 5.
```

4e.  Why is there a difference? _____

_____

_____

_____

_____

_____

_____

_____

_____

5.  In your opinion, approximately what percent of the following kinds of complaints received by the police in your jurisdiction are fabricated:

      (1) CSC                 _____

      (2) Other serious crimes   _____

6a.  Please turn to page 3 in the booklet.  In how many of the CSC cases that you have handled were the victim and assailant acquainted in the following ways?

|  | All | Most | Some | Few | None | DK |
|---|---|---|---|---|---|---|
| (1) Total strangers |  |  |  |  |  |  |
| (2) Casual acquaintances |  |  |  |  |  |  |
| (3) Close acquaintances, but not sexually intimate |  |  |  |  |  |  |
| (4) Close acquaintances, and sexually intimate |  |  |  |  |  |  |
| (5) Members of different races |  |  |  |  |  |  |

6b.  Using approximate numbers, how many cases have you had where:

(1) the victim and assailant were separated spouses? _____

(2) the victim and assailant were members of the same family or household (excluding spouses)? _____

(3) the victim and assailant were members of the same sex? _____

(4) the victim was under 13? _____

INTERVIEWER: IF RESPONDENT HAS NO PRE-CSC LAW EXPERIENCE, CHECK
HERE [ ] ———⟶ GO TO 7c.

6c. Since the new law passed, have you noticed any change in the number
or types     of cases referred to in questions 6a and 6b?

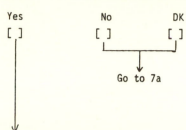

Yes          No          DK
[ ]          [ ]          [ ]

Go to 7a

6d.  Please explain. _____

_____

_____

_____

_____

_____

_____

_____

_____

_____

_____

_____

_____

7a.  Is the amount of plea bargaining that goes on now more, the same, or
     less than before the new CSC law went into effect?

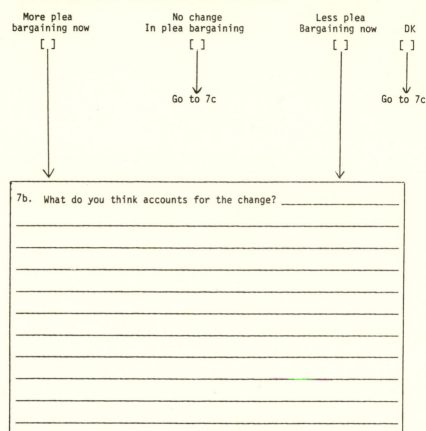

|   More plea      |   No change       |   Less plea      |      |
| bargaining now   | In plea bargaining | Bargaining now   |  DK  |
|      [ ]         |       [ ]         |      [ ]         | [ ]  |
|                  |                   |                  |      |
|                  |   Go to 7c        |                  | Go to 7c |

7b.  What do you think accounts for the change? _____

_____

_____

_____

_____

_____

_____

_____

_____

_____

_____


7c.  In the CSC cases you have handled under the new law, approximately what
     percent of the defendants have pleaded guilty to reduced charges?

                                              _____

7d.  Approximately what percent of the defendents have pleaded guilty to
     negotiated sentences?

                                              _____

7e. How does this compare to the number pled to reduced charges or negotiated sentences in other equally serious crimes? Are there more in CSC, fewer in CSC, or are they about the same?

More in CSC          Fewer in CSC          About the Same          DK
   [ ]                    [ ]                      [ ]                  [ ]
                                                    Go to 8a

7f. In your opinion, why is there a difference? _____

_____

_____

_____

_____

_____

_____

_____

_____

_____

_____

_____

_____

_____

_____

_____

INTERVIEWER: IF RESPONDENT HAS NO PRE-CSC LAW EXPERIENCE, CHECK HERE [ ]
           ⟶   GO TO 9a.

8a.   Have pretrial activities (such as arraignment, preliminary hearing, etc.)
      changed as a result of the new law?

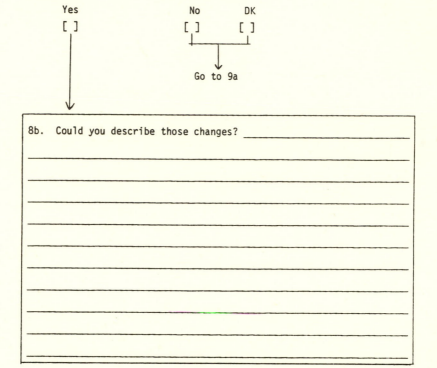

```
         Yes                    No        DK
         [ ]                    [ ]       [ ]
                                |_____|
                                     |
                                     v
                                Go to 9a
```

8b.   Could you describe those changes? _____

_____

_____

_____

_____

_____

_____

_____

_____

_____

8c.   In what percent of CSC cases do you get an opportunity to meet with the
      victim prior to trial?
                                                      _____

8d.   On the average, about how much time are you able to spend with the
      victim?
                                                      _____

9a. Please turn to page 4 in the booklet. This question concerns elements of sexual assault crimes that can influence the outcome of trials. On a scale from 1, meaning absolutely essential, to 7, meaning useless, please check how important the following items are for persuading a jury to convict in sexual assault cases tried under the new law.

|  | Absolutely Essential | | | | | | Useless | |
|---|---|---|---|---|---|---|---|---|
|  | 1 | 2 | 3 | 4 | 5 | 6 | 7 | DK |
| (1) Physical injury of complainant | | | | | | | | |
| (2) Defendent's use of dangerous weapon | | | | | | | | |
| (3) Penetration | | | | | | | | |
| (4) Non-consent of complainant | | | | | | | | |
| (5) Corroborating witnesses | | | | | | | | |
| (6) Resistance of complainant | | | | | | | | |
| (7) Prompt report by complainant | | | | | | | | |
| (8) Complainant's past behavior or reputation | | | | | | | | |
| (9) Lab evidence | | | | | | | | |
| (10) Thorough police investigation | | | | | | | | |
| (11) Victim demeanor | | | | | | | | |
| (12) Outcry of victim | | | | | | | | |

INTERVIEWER:   IF RESPONDENT HAS NO PRE-CSC LAW EXPERIENCE, CHECK HERE [ ]
               ⟶ GO TO 11a.

9b.  Now please turn to page 5 in the booklet.  Using the same list, please
     check how important the following items used to be for persuading a jury
     to convict in sexual assault cases tried before enactment of the CSC law.

| | Absolutely Essential | | | | | | Useless | |
|---|---|---|---|---|---|---|---|---|
| | 1 | 2 | 3 | 4 | 5 | 6 | 7 | DK |
| (1) Physical injury of complainant | | | | | | | | |
| (2) Defendent's use of dangerous weapon | | | | | | | | |
| (3) Penetration | | | | | | | | |
| (4) Non-consent of complainant | | | | | | | | |
| (5) Corroborating witnesses | | | | | | | | |
| (6) Resistance of complainant | | | | | | | | |
| (7) Prompt report by complainant | | | | | | | | |
| (8) Complainant's past behavior or reputation | | | | | | | | |
| (9) Lab evidence | | | | | | | | |
| (10) Thorough police investigation | | | | | | | | |
| (11) Victim demeanor | | | | | | | | |
| (12) Outcry of victim | | | | | | | | |

INTERVIEWER:   IF RESPONDENT HAS NO CSC TRIAL EXPERIENCE, CHECK HERE [ ]
        ⟶ GO TO 10e.

10a.   Have you ever won a case under the new CSC law which you do not think
      you would have won under the previous law?

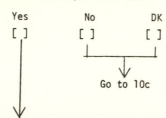

        Yes          No          DK
        [ ]         [ ]       [ ]

Go to 10c

| 10b.   Please briefly describe such cases and explain why: |
| --- |
|  |
|  |
|  |
|  |
|  |

10c.   Have you ever lost a case under the new CSC law which you do not think
      you would have lost under the previous law?

        Yes          No          DK
        [ ]         [ ]       [ ]

Go to 10e

| 10d.   Please briefly describe such cases and explain why: |
| --- |
|  |
|  |
|  |
|  |
|  |

10e.  In general, how have prosecutors chances of winning sexual assault
      cases changed as a result of the new law?  Would you say your chances
      have greatly improved,  improved, stayed about the same, diminished
      or greatly diminished?

| Greatly Improved | Improved | Stayed about the same | Diminished | Greatly Diminished | DK |
|---|---|---|---|---|---|
| [ ] | [ ] | [ ] | [ ] | [ ] | [ ] |

Go to 11a                                                     Go to 11a

10f.  What's the single most important reason for that change?

_____

_____

_____

_____

_____

_____

10g.  Are there any other reasons?

_____

_____

_____

_____

INTERVIEWER: IF RESPONDENT HAS NO CSC TRIAL EXPERIENCE, CHECK HERE [ ]
⟶ GO TO 12a.

11a. How often have <u>in camera</u> hearings been used in the CSC cases you've tried?

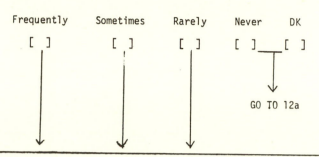

| Frequently | Sometimes | Rarely | Never | DK |
|:---:|:---:|:---:|:---:|:---:|
| [ ] | [ ] | [ ] | [ ] | [ ] |

GO TO 12a

11b. What is the most common reason for these hearings?

_____

_____

_____

_____

_____

11c. What is usually the outcome of these hearings?

_____

_____

_____

_____

_____

INTERVIEWER:   IF RESPONDENT HAS NO PRE-CSC EXPERIENCE, CHECK HERE [ ]
                ────→  GO TO 13a

12a. Have you changed your courtroom tactics  or strategies for prosecuting
     sexual assault cases since the new CSC law went into effect?

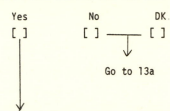

```
            Yes            No            DK.
            [ ]            [ ] ──┬── [ ]
                                 │
                                 ↓
                            Go to 13a
```

┌─────────────────────────────────────────────────────────────────────┐
│                                                                       │
│   12b.   Please explain why and how: _____  │
│   _____ │
│   _____ │
│   _____ │
│   _____ │
│   _____ │
│   _____ │
│   _____ │
│   _____ │
│   _____ │
│   _____ │
│   _____ │
│   _____ │
│   _____ │
│   _____ │
│   _____ │
│   _____ │
│                                                                       │
└─────────────────────────────────────────────────────────────────────┘

13a.  How much can a judge's discretion control the outcome of a CSC jury
      trial?  Can he control the outcome completely, a great deal, somewhat,
      very little, or not at all?

|            |              |          | Very   |            |    |
|------------|--------------|----------|--------|------------|----|
| Completely | A great deal | Somewhat | Little | Not at all | DK |
| [ ]        | [ ]          | [ ]      | [ ]    | [ ]        | [ ] → Go to 13c |

13b.  Please explain:  _____

      _____

      _____

      _____

      _____

      _____

      _____


INTERVIEWER:   IF RESPONDENT HAS NO PRE-CSC LAW EXPERIENCE, CHECK HERE [ ]
               ──→ GO TO 13e


13c.  Has the new law changed the amount of discretion a judge has in a
      sexual assault jury trial?

                        Yes          No          DK
                        [ ]          [ ] ──┬── [ ]
                                           ↓
                                      GO TO 13e



      ┌─────────────────────────────────────────────────────────────────┐
      │  13d.  In what way?  _____     │
      │                                                                   │
      │  _____ │
      │                                                                   │
      │  _____ │
      │                                                                   │
      │  _____ │
      │                                                                   │
      │  _____ │
      │                                                                   │
      │  _____ │
      │                                                                   │
      │  _____ │
      └─────────────────────────────────────────────────────────────────┘

13e.  Have you ever prosecuted a sexual assault case in which you believed
      the judge's discretion actually changed the outcome of a sexual assault
      jury trial?

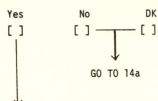

            Yes              No            DK

            [ ]              [ ] ——————— [ ]

                                    |
                                    ↓

                              GO TO 14a

    ┌──────────────────────────────────────────────────────────────┐
    │                                                                │
    │  13f.  Please explain and describe each case. _____  │
    │  _____  │
    │  _____  │
    │  _____  │
    │  _____  │
    │  _____  │
    │  _____  │
    │  _____  │
    │  _____  │
    │  _____  │
    │  _____  │
    │  _____  │
    │  _____  │
    │  _____  │
    │  _____  │
    │  _____  │
    │  _____  │
    │  _____  │
    │  _____  │
    └──────────────────────────────────────────────────────────────┘

INTERVIEWER:  IF RESPONDENT HAS NO PRE-CSC LAW EXPERIENCE, CHECK HERE [ ]
⟶ GO TO 14f.

14a. Overall, do you believe a sexual assault victim's experience in the criminal
justice system has become more or less traumatic under the new law?  Would
you say a victim's experience now is much more traumatic, more traumatic,
unchanged, less traumatic, or much less traumatic?

| Much more traumatic | More traumatic | Unchanged | Less traumatic | Much less traumatic | DK |
|:---:|:---:|:---:|:---:|:---:|:---:|
| [ ] | [ ] | [ ] | [ ] | [ ] | [ ] |

Go to 14e          Go to 14f                              Go to 14f

14b.  Please refer to page  6 and check how much each of these factors
has contributed to this improvement.

| | Greatly | Some | Very Little | None | DK |
|---|---|---|---|---|---|
| (1) Restriction on past sexual history evidence | | | | | |
| (2) No need to prove non-consent | | | | | |
| (3) No need to prove resistance | | | | | |
| (4) Crisis Center support | | | | | |
| (5) Changed social attitudes about women and rape | | | | | |
| (6) Treatment of victim by police | | | | | |
| (7) Women police assigned to sexual assault cases | | | | | |
| (8) Treatment of victim by hospital personnel | | | | | |
| (9) Coverage of cases by news media | | | | | |
| (10) Other factors: (list) | | | | | |

14c.  Which one of these factors is most important? _____

_____

_____


14d.  Do you ever tell complainants or have your subordinates tell complainants
      that the new law will make their experience less onerous in order to
      encourage them to prosecute?  Do you tell them always, frequently,
      sometimes, rarely, or never?

|       |            |           |        |       | Not        |
| Always | Frequently | Sometimes | Rarely | Never | Applicable |
| [ ]   | [ ]        | [ ]       | [ ]    | [ ]   | [ ]        |

      INTERVIEWER: FOR RESPONDENTS WHO ARE ASKED 14d. - SKIP 14e. ———> GO TO 14f.

14e.  Please explain why this experience is worse now. _____

_____

_____

_____

_____

_____


14f.  How could the victim's experience in the criminal justice system be
      improved?

_____

_____

_____

_____

_____

_____

_____

15a. Do you think the new CSC law violates defendants' Constitutional rights?
Would you say the law definitely violates them, probably violates them,
probably does not violate them, or definitely does not violate them?

| Definitely<br>Violates<br>Them | Probably<br>Violates<br>Them | Probably Does<br>Not Violate<br>Them | Definitely Does<br>Not Violate<br>Them | DK |
|:---:|:---:|:---:|:---:|:---:|
| [ ] | [ ] | [ ] | [ ] | [ ] |

GO TO 16a

15b.  Please explain: _____

_____

_____

_____

_____

_____

_____

_____

_____

_____

_____

_____

_____

_____

16a.  Would you make any changes in the new law?

| Yes | No | DK |
|-----|-----|-----|
| [ ] | [ ] ——┬—— [ ] |

GO TO 16c

16b.  What changes? _____

_____

_____

_____

_____

_____

_____


16c.  Do you think this law was necessary?

| Yes | No | DK |
|-----|-----|-----|
| [ ] | [ ] ——┬—— [ ] |

GO TO 17a

16d.  Please explain: _____

_____

_____

_____

_____

_____

_____

17a. Does your office have any formal or informal rules, policies, or procedures concerning the handling of CSC cases which are different from those you use to handle equally serious crime?

|        Yes        |     No     |    DK    |
|        [ ]        |     [ ]    |    [ ]    |

GO TO 18a

17b. What are they? _____

_____

_____

_____

_____

_____

_____

_____

_____

_____

_____

_____

_____

17c. Why are they different? _____

_____

_____

_____

_____

_____

_____

18a.   Please turn to page  7 in the booklet.  Recent statistics indicate
       that reports of rape in Michigan are increasing.  What do you think is
       responsible for the increase?  On this list, please check the 3 most
       important reasons for this increase.

       (1)   [ ]   Sexual permissiveness

       (2)   [ ]   More reporting because of increased convictions

       (3)   [ ]   Effect of the new CSC law

       (4)   [ ]   General increase in violence

       (5)   [ ]   More reporting because of increased sensitivity of criminal
                   justice system

       (6)   [ ]   Influence of pornography

       (7)   [ ]   Women's liberation

       (8)   [ ]   More reporting because of a change in public attitude
                   toward rape

       (9)   [ ]   Racial tensions

      (10)   [ ]   Other (specify) _____

             _____

             _____


18b.   Which one of these reasons is most important?   _____

       _____

       _____

## Part II

Please turn to pages 8 and 9 in the booklet. The following are different ways to view the new CSC law and the events leading up to its passage. Place an X on the scale point which best reflects your position.

1.          POSITION A                              POSITION B

Judges are likely to exercise            Judges exercise discretion equally
discretion in CSC cases more often       in the handling of all types of
than in cases involving other            serious crimes.
serious crimes.

A_____+_____+_____+_____B

2.          POSITION A                              POSITION B

Any significant changes in the           Only explicit legal reforms such
handling of rape cases over the last     as those contained in the new
few years would have come about with     CSC law could bring about
or without the new law.                  significant changes in the handling
                                         of rape cases.

A_____+_____+_____+_____B

3.          POSITION A                              POSITION B

As long as we have the kind of           Sexual assaults upon women are the
society we do, women are going to        acts of deviant individuals and
be sexually assaulted.                   reflect little, if anything,
                                         about the larger society.

A_____+_____+_____+_____B

4.          POSITION A                              POSITION B

The possibility of being overturned      The possibility of appeal does not
on appeal greatly influences             influence judicial behavior in CSC
judicial behavior in CSC cases.          cases

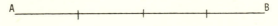

A_____+_____+_____+_____B

5.          POSITION A                              POSITION B

The passage of the new CSC law is        The new CSC law will have very
likely to foster broad changes in        little impact on public
the way society thinks about the         opinion.
crime of rape.

A_____+_____+_____+_____B

6.            POSITION A                          POSITION B

Pressure from community groups          The criminal justice system must
should influence the workings           be immune to community pressure
of the criminal justice system.         in the pursuit of justice.

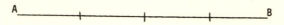

7.            POSITION A                          POSITION B

The passage of the new CSC law is       More than anything else, the
an outgrowth of genuine concern         passage of the new CSC law
about the crime of rape and the         represents a successful power
inadequacy of the previous statutes     play by feminists groups.  Their
for dealing with it.                    victory is a lesson in symbolic
                                        politics.

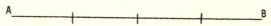

8.            POSITION A                          POSITION B

Regardless of what legal officials      Rape is a special kind of crime.
think about the new CSC law, they       Simply changing the laws will not
can be expected to comply with its      guarantee compliance on the part
implementation.                         of those who handle and process
                                        such cases through the legal system.

## Part III

1.  Please turn to page 10 in the booklet.  In your opinion, which crimes
    should receive the severest sentence?  Rank the following in order,
    placing a 1 by the crime which should receive the severest sentence,
    a 2 by the crime you think should be second and so on.

    _____  aggravated assault

    _____  vandalism

    _____  breaking and entering, occupied dwelling

    _____  CSC 3

    _____  attempted murder

    _____  looting

    _____  CSC 1

    _____  auto theft

Now, using the scale on page 11 in the booklet, please tell me if you agree
strongly, agree, disagree or disagree strongly with the following statements.

2.  Rape is a crime of violence, not passion.

    | Agree strongly | Agree | Disagree | Disagree Strongly | DK |
    |:---:|:---:|:---:|:---:|:---:|
    | [ ] | [ ] | [ ] | [ ] | [ ] |

3.  Most women can successfully resist being raped if they really want to.

    | Agree strongly | Agree | Disagree | Disagree Strongly | DK |
    |:---:|:---:|:---:|:---:|:---:|
    | [ ] | [ ] | [ ] | [ ] | [ ] |

4.  At least 10% of CSC victims provoke the attack by their appearance and
    behavior.

    | Agree strongly | Agree | Disagree | Disagree Strongly | DK |
    |:---:|:---:|:---:|:---:|:---:|
    | [ ] | [ ] | [ ] | [ ] | [ ] |

5.  The Women's Movement is working for needed change in American society.

    | Agree strongly | Agree | Disagree | Disagree strongly | DK |
    |:---:|:---:|:---:|:---:|:---:|
    | [ ] | [ ] | [ ] | [ ] | [ ] |

6.  The best way to decrease the frequency of rape is for women to learn to avoid dangerous situations.

    Agree strongly    Agree    Disagree    Disagree strongly    DK
         [ ]            [ ]       [ ]             [ ]            [ ]

7.  The death penalty should be reinstated in Michigan.

    Agree strongly    Agree    Disagree    Disagree strongly    DK
         [ ]            [ ]       [ ]             [ ]            [ ]

8.  Would you describe your own political views as conservative, moderate, liberal or radical?

    Conservative    Moderate    Liberal    Radical    DK
        [ ]           [ ]         [ ]        [ ]       L ]

Part IV

Now, please turn to page 12 in the booklet and read the scenario presented there. When you are through, I will ask you a few questions about it.

A. Suppose the police receive a rape complaint, conduct an investigation, and conclude that the following had occurred: An 18-year old girl went to a drive-in movie with a 20-year old boy whom she'd been dating for several months and with whom she had had intercourse on several occasions. They drank a six-pack of beer and climbed into the back seat, where they began petting heavily. As the boy started to remove her clothes, the girl said she didn't want to go any further. He took her "No" to be a teasing "Yes" and became more persistant. She resisted, but eventually gave in. After intercourse, she was upset, demanded to be taken home, and called the police.

INTERVIEWER:  ONCE THE RESPONDENT REPLIES "Yes" TO AN "a" or "b" QUESTION,
              DISCONTINUE ASKING IT IN SUBSEQUENT VERSIONS. Ask "c" and
              "d" QUESTIONS UNTIL RESPONDENT REPLIES "Yes" TO A "d" QUESTION,
              THEN ———⟶ GO TO SCENARIO B.

1.  (a)  Would the police in your jurisdiction be likely    [ ] Yes  [ ] No ——⟶ Go to
         to bring this case to your attention?                                  2(a)

    (b)  Would you be likely to issue a warrant?           [ ] Yes  [ ] No ——⟶ Go to
                                                                                2(a)

    (c)  At what charge?                                    _____

    (d)  Do you think you could get a conviction in
         a jury trial?                                      [ ] Yes  [ ] No

2.  Suppose they had not been drinking, and the incident took place in the front seat of the car.

    (a)  Would the police be likely to bring the case to
         your attention?                                    [ ] Yes  [ ] No ——⟶ Go to
                                                                                3(a)

    (b)  Would you be likely to issue a warrant?           [ ] Yes  [ ] No ——⟶ Go to
                                                                                3(a)

    (c)  At what charge?                                    _____

    (d)  Do you think you could get a conviction in
         a jury trial?                                      [ ] Yes  [ ] No

3.  What if it had been their first date, in addition to the fact that they had not been drinking and the incident occurred in the front seat?

    (a)  Would the police be likely to bring it to you?    [ ] Yes  [ ] No ——⟶ Go to
                                                                                4(a)

    (b)  Would you be likely to issue a warrant?           [ ] Yes  [ ] No ——⟶ Go to
                                                                                4(a)

    (c)  At what charge?                                    _____

    (d)  Do you think you could win a jury trial?          [ ] Yes  [ ] No

4. How about if, in addition to the changes I've just described, she
   claimed he struck her and she had clearly visible bruises on her face?

   (a) Would the police be likely to bring the case to you?   [ ] Yes   [ ] No ⟶ Go to
                                                                                   B

   (b) Would you be likely to issue a warrant?                [ ] Yes   [ ] No ⟶ Go to
                                                                                   B

   (c) At what charge?                                        _____

   (d) Do you think you could win a jury trial?               ['] Yes   [ ] No


Now, please turn to page 13 in the booklet and read the scenario there. When
you are through, I will again ask you a few questions.

B. Imagine that in another case a 30-year old secretary complained to the
   police that after an office party, her 40-year old boss pinched her
   buttocks, pushed her up against a filing cabinet and fondled her breasts.
   After questioning her further, the police determine that they had been
   lovers some time in the past, that they had been drinking and flirting
   at the party, and that the man had stopped and apologized when the woman
   protested.

INTERVIEWER:   ONCE THE RESPONDENT REPLIES "Yes" TO AN "a" OR "b" QUESTION,
               DISCONTINUE ASKING IT IN SUBSEQUENT VERSIONS.  ASK "c" and "d"
               UNTIL RESPONDENT REPLIES "Yes" TO A "d" QUESTION, THEN ⟶ GO TO PART V.

1. (a) Would the police be likely to bring this case
       to your attention?                                     [ ] Yes   [ ] No ⟶ Go to
                                                                                   2(a)

   (b) Would you be likely to issue a warrant?                [ ] Yes   [ ] No ⟶ Go to
                                                                                   2(a)

   (c) At what charge?                                        _____

   (d) Do you think you could get a conviction at a
       jury trial?                                            [ ] Yes   [ ] No

2. Suppose they had not been lovers in the past.

   (a) Would the police be likely to bring this case
       to your attention?                                     [ ] Yes   [ ] No ⟶ Go to
                                                                                   3(a)

   (b) Would you be likely to issue a warrant?                [ ] Yes   [ ] No ⟶ Go to
                                                                                   3(a)

   (c) At what charge?                                        _____

   (d) Do you think you could get a conviction at a
       jury trial?                                            [ ] Yes   [ ] No

3. Suppose that in addition to not having been lovers, the incident occurred after the secretary had worked late at her employer's request, rather than after a party.

    (a) Would the police then be likely to bring the case to you?     [ ] Yes  [ ] No  ⟶ Go to 4(a)

    (b) Would you be likely to issue a warrant?     [ ] Yes  [ ] No  ⟶ Go to 4(a)

    (c) At what charge?     _____

    (d) Do you think you could get a conviction?     [ ] Yes  [ ] No

4. What if this had been the most recent of a series of similar events, and the man had been threatening to fire her if she did not have sex with him.

    (a) Would the police be likely to bring the case to you?     [ ] Yes  [ ] No  ⟶ Go to Part V

    (b) Would you be likely to issue a warrant?     [ ] Yes  [ ] No  ⟶ Go to Part V

    (c) At what charge?     _____

    (d) Do you think you could get a conviction?     [ ] Yes  [ ] No

Part V

A.  ORGANIZATIONS

What are the names of the organizations which are involved in handling sexual assault problems in your county?

_____

_____

_____

_____

_____

_____

_____

_____

_____

_____

_____

_____

_____

_____

_____


B.  ASSAULT CRISIS CENTER

Now using the scale on page 14 in the booklet, please tell me if the following occur in every case, in most cases, in some cases, in rare cases or never.

1.  When you handle sexual assault cases, how often do you work with an assault crisis center.

| in every case | in most cases | in some cases | in rare cases | never | DK |
|---------------|---------------|---------------|---------------|-------|-----|
| [ ] | [ ] | [ ] | [ ] | [ ] | [ ] |

Go to C

B.  ASSAULT CRISIS CENTER (Continued)

2.  When you need information or help in a sexual assault case, do you
    know someone personally to contact at an assault crisis center?

        Yes             No              DK
        [ ]             [ ]             [ ]

3.  When you work with an assault crisis center, how often do you initiate
    the contacts?

    in every     in most      in some      in rare
      case        cases        cases        cases      never       DK
      [ ]          [ ]          [ ]          [ ]        [ ]        [ ]

4.  How often do you have difficulty coordinating the activities or
    services of your office and assault crisis centers?

    in every     in most      in some      in rare
      case        cases        cases        cases      never       DK
      [ ]          [ ]          [ ]          [ ]        [ ]        [ ]

5.  How often do you feel dissatisfied with the way assault crisis centers
    handle a case?

    in every     in most      in some      in rare
      case        cases        cases        cases      never       DK
      [ ]          [ ]          [ ]          [ ]        [ ]        [ ]

6.  How often do you think the assault crisis centers feel dissatisfied
    with the way your office handles a case?

    in every     in most      in some      in rare
      case        cases        cases        cases      never       DK
      [ ]          [ ]          [ ]          [ ]        [ ]        [ ]

7.  What was the most serious conflict or disagreement you can recall
    your office having with an assault crisis center.

    _____

    _____

    _____

    _____

C.  HOSPITAL

    1.  When you handle sexual assault cases, how often do you work with a
        hospital or other medical facility?

| in every<br>case | in most<br>cases | in some<br>cases | in rare<br>cases | never | DK |
|:---:|:---:|:---:|:---:|:---:|:---:|
| [ ] | [ ] | [ ] | [ ] | [ ] | [ ] |

                                                                                            Go to D

    2.  When you need information or help in a sexual assault case, do you
        know someone personally to contact at a hospital?

| Yes | No | DK |
|:---:|:---:|:---:|
| [ ] | [ ] | [ ] |

    3.  How often do you have difficulty coordinating the activities or
        services of your office and a hospital?

| in every<br>case | in most<br>cases | in some<br>cases | in rare<br>cases | never | DK |
|:---:|:---:|:---:|:---:|:---:|:---:|
| [ ] | [ ] | [ ] | [ ] | [ ] | [ ] |

    4.  How often do you feel dissatisfied with the way hospitals handle
        a case?

| in every<br>case | in most<br>cases | in some<br>cases | in rare<br>cases | never | DK |
|:---:|:---:|:---:|:---:|:---:|:---:|
| [ ] | [ ] | [ ] | [ ] | [ ] | [ ] |

    5.  What was the most serious conflict or disagreement you can recall
        your office having with a hospital?

_____

_____

_____

_____

_____

_____

_____

_____

D.  MEDIA

1.  When you handle sexual assault cases, how often do you have contact
    with the media?

| in every<br>case | in most<br>cases | in some<br>cases | in rare<br>cases | never | DK |
|:---:|:---:|:---:|:---:|:---:|:---:|
| [ ] | [ ] | [ ] | [ ] | [ ] | [ ] |

Go to E

2.  When you need information or help in a sexual assault case, do you
    know someone personally to contact in the media?

| Yes | No | DK |
|:---:|:---:|:---:|
| [ ] | [ ] | [ ] |

3.  How often do you feel dissatisfied with the way media covers a sexual
    assault case?

| in every<br>case | in most<br>cases | in some<br>cases | in rare<br>cases | never | DK |
|:---:|:---:|:---:|:---:|:---:|:---:|
| [ ] | [ ] | [ ] | [ ] | [ ] | [ ] |

4.  How often do you think the media feel dissatisfied with the way your
    office handles a case?

| in every<br>case | in most<br>cases | in some<br>cases | in rare<br>cases | never | DK |
|:---:|:---:|:---:|:---:|:---:|:---:|
| [ ] | [ ] | [ ] | [ ] | [ ] | [ ] |

5.  What was the most serious conflict or disagreement you can recall
    your office having with the media.

    _____

    _____

    _____

    _____

    _____

    _____

E.  POLICE

1.  How often do you have difficulty coordinating the activities or services of your office and the police?

| in every case | in most cases | in some cases | in rare cases | never | DK |
|:---:|:---:|:---:|:---:|:---:|:---:|
| [ ] | [ ] | [ ] | [ ] | [ ] | [ ] |

                                                                    Go to F

2.  How often do you feel dissatisfied with the way the police handle a sexual assault case?

| in every case | in most cases | in some cases | in rare cases | never | DK |
|:---:|:---:|:---:|:---:|:---:|:---:|
| [ ] | [ ] | [ ] | [ ] | [ ] | [ ] |

3.  How often do you think the police feel dissatisfied with the way your office handles a case?

| in every case | in most cases | in some cases | in rare cases | never | DK |
|:---:|:---:|:---:|:---:|:---:|:---:|
| [ ] | [ ] | [ ] | [ ] | [ ] | [ ] |

4.  What was the most serious conflict or disagreement you can recall your office having with the police?

_____

_____

_____

_____

_____

_____

_____

_____

_____

_____

_____

_____

F. SERVICES NEEDED

   1. Are there services not being provided for sexual assault victims in your county that should be made available?

                    Yes                   No

                    [ ]                 [ ] ⟶ Go to Part VI

   2. What are they? _____

_____

_____

_____

_____

_____

_____

_____

_____

_____

_____

_____

_____

Part VI

1.  How long have you been a prosecutor? _____

2.  Approximately, what is the total number of sexual asssault cases in which you have played a role during your career as a prosecutor? _____

3.  Of this number, how many have you handled since the new CSC law went into effect? _____

    Approximately how many of each of the following have you either handled personally or supervised?

    |  | Cases handled or supervised |
    |---|---|
    | 4. Warrant decision in a sexual assault case before the new law? | _____ |
    | 5. Warrant decision in a sexual assault case after the new law? | _____ |
    | 6. Warrant decision for other equally serious crimes? | _____ |
    | 7. Trial of a sexual assault case before the new law? | _____ |
    | 8. Trial of a sexual assault case after the new law? | _____ |
    | 9. Trial of another equally serious crime? | _____ |

Part VII

Is there anything about the new law you care to add? _____

_____

_____

_____

_____

# THE LAW

Act No. 266
Public Acts of 1974
Approved by Governor
August 12, 1974

## STATE OF MICHIGAN
## 77TH LEGISLATURE
## REGULAR SESSION OF 1974

Introduced by Senators Byker, Faust, Zaagman, Hart, Lodge, Bowman, Toepp, Novak, Pursell, Plawecki, Mack, McCauley, Zollar, O'Brien, Cartwright, Rozycki, Davis, Bouwsma, Brown, DeGrow, Rockwell, Richardson, Ballenger, Faxon, Cooper, McCollough, DeMaso, Pittenger, Bishop and Fleming

## ENROLLED SENATE BILL No. 1207

AN ACT to amend Act No. 328 of the Public Acts of 1931, entitled "An act to revise, consolidate, codify and add to the statutes relating to crimes; to define crimes and prescribe the penalties therefor; to provide for the competency of evidence at the trial of persons accused of crime; to provide immunity from prosecution for certain witnesses appearing at such trials; and to repeal certain acts and parts of acts inconsistent with or contravening any of the provisions of this act," as amended, being sections 750.1 to 750.568 of the Compiled Laws of 1970, by adding sections 520a, 520b, 520c, 520d, 520e, 520f, 520g, 520h, 520i, 520j, 520k and 520l; and to repeal certain acts and parts of acts.

*The People of the State of Michigan enact:*

Section 1. Act No. 328 of the Public Acts of 1931, as amended, being sections 750.1 to 750.568 of the Compiled Laws of 1970, is amended by adding sections 520a, 520b, 520c, 520d, 520e, 520f, 520g, 520h, 520i, 520j, 520k and 520l to read as follows:

Sec. 520a. As used in sections 520a to 520l:

(a) "Actor" means a person accused of criminal sexual conduct.

(b) "Intimate parts" includes the primary genital area, groin, inner thigh, buttock, or breast of a human being.

(c) "Mentally defective" means that a person suffers from a mental disease or defect which renders that person temporarily or permanently incapable of appraising the nature of his or her conduct.

(d) "Mentally incapacitated" means that a person is rendered temporarily incapable of appraising or controlling his or her conduct due to the influence of a narcotic, anesthetic, or other substance administered to that person without his or her consent, or due to any other act committed upon that person without his or her consent.

(e) "Physically helpless" means that a person is unconscious, asleep, or for any other reason is physically unable to communicate unwillingness to an act.

(f) "Personal injury" means bodily injury, disfigurement, mental anguish, chronic pain, pregnancy, disease, or loss or impairment of a sexual or reproductive organ.

(g) "Sexual contact" includes the intentional touching of the victim's or actor's intimate parts or the intentional touching of the clothing covering the immediate area of the victim's or actor's intimate parts, if that intentional touching can reasonably be construed as being for the purpose of sexual arousal or gratification.

(h) "Sexual penetration" means sexual intercourse, cunnilingus, fellatio, anal intercourse, or any other intrusion, however slight, of any part of a person's body or of any object into the genital or anal openings of another person's body, but emission of semen is not required.

(i) "Victim" means the person alleging to have been subjected to criminal sexual conduct.

Sec. 520b. (1) A person is guilty of criminal sexual conduct in the first degree if he or she engages in sexual penetration with another person and if any of the following circumstances exists:

(a) That other person is under 13 years of age.

(b) The other person is at least 13 but less than 16 years of age and the actor is a member of the same household as the victim, the actor is related to the victim by blood or affinity to the fourth degree to the victim, or the actor is in a position of authority over the victim and used this authority to coerce the victim to submit.

(c) Sexual penetration occurs under circumstances involving the commission of any other felony.

(d) The actor is aided or abetted by 1 or more other persons and either of the following circumstances exists:

(i) The actor knows or has reason to know that the victim is mentally defective, mentally incapacitated or physically helpless.

(ii) The actor uses force or coercion to accomplish the sexual penetration. Force or coercion includes but is not limited to any of the circumstances listed in subdivision (f) (i) to (v).

(e) The actor is armed with a weapon or any article used or fashioned in a manner to lead the victim to reasonably believe it to be a weapon.

(f) The actor causes personal injury to the victim and force or coercion is used to accomplish sexual penetration. Force or coercion includes but is not limited to any of the following circumstances:

(i) When the actor overcomes the victim through the actual application of physical force or physical violence.

(ii) When the actor coerces the victim to submit by threatening to use force or violence on the victim, and the victim believes that the actor has the present ability to execute these threats.

(iii) When the actor coerces the victim to submit by threatening to retaliate in the future against the victim, or any other person, and the victim believes that the actor has the ability to execute this threat. As used in this subdivision, "to retaliate" includes threats of physical punishment, kidnapping, or extortion.

(iv) When the actor engages in the medical treatment or examination of the victim in a manner or for purposes which are medically recognized as unethical or unacceptable.

(v) When the actor, through concealment or by the element of surprise, is able to overcome the victim.

(g) The actor causes personal injury to the victim, and the actor knows or has reason to know that the victim is mentally defective, mentally incapacitated, or physically helpless.

(2) Criminal sexual conduct in the first degree is a felony punishable by imprisonment in the state prison for life or for any term of years.

Sec. 520c. (1) A person is guilty of criminal sexual conduct in the second degree if the person engages in sexual contact with another person and if any of the following circumstances exists:

(a) That other person is under 13 years of age.

(b) That other person is at least 13 but less than 16 years of age and the actor is a member of the same household as the victim, or is related by blood or affinity to the fourth degree to the victim, or is in a position of authority over the victim and the actor used this authority to coerce the victim to submit.

(c) Sexual contact occurs under circumstances involving the commission of any other felony.

(d) The actor is aided or abetted by 1 or more other persons and either of the following circumstances exists:

(i) The actor knows or has reason to know that the victim is mentally defective, mentally incapacitated or physically helpless.

(ii) The actor uses force or coercion to accomplish the sexual contact. Force or coercion includes but is not limited to any of the circumstances listed in sections 520b (1) (f) (i) to (v).

(e) The actor is armed with a weapon, or any article used or fashioned in a manner to lead a person to reasonably believe it to be a weapon.

(f) The actor causes personal injury to the victim and force or coercion is used to accomplish the sexual contact. Force or coercion includes but is not limited to any of the circumstances listed in section 520b (1) (f) (i) to (v).

(g) The actor causes personal injury to the victim and the actor knows or has reason to know that the victim is mentally defective, mentally incapacitated, or physically helpless.

(2) Criminal sexual conduct in the second degree is a felony punishable by imprisonment for not more than 15 years.

Sec. 520d. (1) A person is guilty of criminal sexual conduct in the third degree if the person engages in sexual penetration with another person and if any of the following circumstances exists:

(a) That other person is at least 13 years of age and under 16 years of age.

(b) Force or coercion is used to accomplish the sexual penetration. Force or coercion includes but is not limited to any of the circumstances listed in section 520b (1) (f) (i) to (v).

(c) The actor knows or has reason to know that the victim is mentally defective, mentally incapacitated, or physically helpless.

(2) Criminal sexual conduct in the third degree is a felony punishable by imprisonment for not more than 15 years.

Sec. 520e. (1) A person is guilty of criminal sexual conduct in the fourth degree if he or she engages in sexual contact with another person and if either of the following circumstances exists:

(a) Force or coercion is used to accomplish the sexual contact. Force or coercion includes but is not limited to any of the circumstances listed in section 520b (1) (f) (i) to (iv).

(b) The actor knows or has reason to know that the victim is mentally defective, mentally incapacitated, or physically helpless.

(2) Criminal sexual conduct in the fourth degree is a misdemeanor punishable by imprisonment for not more than 2 years, or by a fine of not more than $500.00, or both.

Sec. 520f. (1) If a person is convicted of a second or subsequent offense under section 520b, 520c, or 520d, the sentence imposed under those sections for the second or subsequent offense shall provide for a mandatory minimum sentence of at least 5 years.

(2) For purposes of this section, an offense is considered a second or subsequent offense if, prior to conviction of the second or subsequent offense, the actor has at any time been convicted under section 520b, 520c, or 520d or under any similar statute of the United States or any state for a criminal sexual offense including rape, carnal knowledge, indecent liberties, gross indecency, or an attempt to commit such an offense.

Sec. 520g. (1) Assault with intent to commit criminal sexual conduct involving sexual penetration shall be a felony punishable by imprisonment for not more than 10 years.

(2) Assault with intent to commit criminal sexual conduct in the second degree is a felony punishable by imprisonment for not more than 5 years.

Sec. 520h. The testimony of a victim need not be corroborated in prosecutions under sections 520b to 520g.

Sec. 520i. A victim need not resist the actor in prosecution under sections 520b to 520g.

Sec. 520j. (1) Evidence of specific instances of the victim's sexual conduct, opinion evidence of the victim's sexual conduct, and reputation evidence of the victim's sexual conduct shall not be admitted under sections 520b to 520g unless and only to the extent that the judge finds that the following proposed evidence is material to a fact at issue in the case and that its inflammatory or prejudicial nature does not outweigh its probative value:

(a) Evidence of the victim's past sexual conduct with the actor.

(b) Evidence of specific instances of sexual activity showing the source or origin of semen, pregnancy, or disease.

(2) If the defendant proposes to offer evidence described in subsection (1) (a) or (b), the defendant within 10 days after the arraignment on the information shall file a written motion and offer of proof. The court may order an *in-camera* hearing to determine whether the

proposed evidence is admissible under subsection (1). If new information is discovered during the course of the trial that may make the evidence described in subsection (1) (a) or (b) admissible, the judge may order an *in-camera* hearing to determine whether the proposed evidence is admissible under subsection (1).

Sec. 520k. Upon the request of the counsel or the victim or actor in a prosecution under sections 520b to 520g the magistrate before whom any person is brought on a charge of having committed an offense under sections 520b to 520g shall order that the names of the victim and actor and details of the alleged offense be suppressed until such time as the actor is arraigned on the information, the charge is dismissed, or the case is otherwise concluded, whichever occurs first.

Sec. 520l. A person does not commit sexual assault under this act if the victim is his or her legal spouse, unless the couple are living apart and one of them has filed for separate maintenance or divorce.

Section 2. All proceedings pending and all rights and liabilities existing, acquired, or incurred at the time this amendatory act takes effect are saved and may be consummated according to the law in force when they are commenced. This amendatory act shall not be construed to affect any prosecution pending or begun before the effective date of this amendatory act.

Section 3. Sections 85, 333, 336, 339, 340, 341, 342 and 520 of Act No. 328 of the Public Acts of 1931, being sections 750.85, 750.333, 750.336, 750.339, 750.340, 750.341, 750.342 and 750.520 of the Compiled Laws of 1970, and section 82 of chapter 7 of Act No. 175 of the Public Acts of 1927, being section 767.82 of the Compiled Laws of 1970, are repealed.

Section 4. This amendatory act shall take effect November 1, 1974.

.............................
Secretary of the Senate.

.............................................
Clerk of the House of Representatives.

Approved......................

.................................
Governor.

# INDEX